REPUBLICA DE CUBA

NAT SHERMAN

25 TOROS 25
HAND MADE

R

HOYO DE MONTERREY
Double Corona
English Market Selection

Suntouso   Hecho A Ma

PARTAGAS
25 · DUNHILL SELECCION SUPREMA No. 12

MONTECRIS

DE TABACOS DE PARTAGAS Y CA. HARANA   ACOS DE PAR

PARTAGAS
25 · LUSITANIA

La Habana, Cuba

RUZ 25 DUNHILL NATURAL
CLARO Nº 220

ROMEO Y JULIETA
25 · PERFECTOS

HOYO
DE MONTERREY

ONTECRISTO 25 · Montecristo No. 5 HABANA

REPU

H. UPMANN
25 · LONSDALES

R·J·
PARK LANE

TELEGRAPH

PUNCH

HABANA   HABANA   HABANA

BOLIVAR
25 · CORONAS GIGANTES Made by Hand

BOLIVAR   BOLIVAR   BOLIVAR

THE CIGAR

THE CIGAR

BARNABY CONRAD III

CHRONICLE BOOKS

SAN FRANCISCO

Dedication:

For John Crichton

My stepfather and friend

Library of Congress Cataloging-in-Publication Data
available.
ISBN: 0-8118-1449-1

Distributed in Canada by Raincoast Books,
8680 Cambie Street
Vancouver, B.C., V6P 6M9

10 9 8 7 6 5 4 3 2 1

Chronicle Books
275 Fifth Street
San Francisco, CA 94103

Chronicle Books® is registered in the US Patent and
Trademark Office.

Acknowledgments:
I would like to thank the following for their support on this project:
Martin Muller of Modernism Gallery; John Berggruen of the Berggruen Gallery; Dale DeGroff of the
Rainbow Room; Nion McEvoy, Michael Carabetta, Charlotte Stone, and Christina Wilson of
Chronicle Books; Curtis Post of The Occidental Grill; Michael Pelusi and Guiseppe Scimeca of Alfred
Dunhill, San Francisco; Tyrrell Connor of Davidoff of Geneva, Larry Sherman of Nat Sherman
International; Nissa Berkebile of Georgetown Tobacco; Carlos Fuente, Jr., and Fred Zaniboni of Arturo
Fuente; Trinidad Cigar Emporio Ltd.; Dan Niccoletta, Tony Muller, Keith Lucero, and Ken Peterson of
Grant's Tobacconists; Scott Rosner of Man's World; Jocelyn Clapp of The Bettmann Archive; Allan
Reuben of Culver Pictures; Mike Pitkow of Ashton Cigars; Robert Wagg of The Cigars of Honduras;
Sherwin Selzer of Danby-Palicio; Steve Wall of Thomas Hinds; Bill Sleig of Club Imports; Allan
Edwards of Hollco-Rohr; Aleli Calso of Lignum-2 Inc.; Rosita Boruchin of Mikes Cigars; Eric Gravell,
Michael Caruso, Dennis Hill, and Ken Krone; Dr. Robert Rothberg; Jill Frish of *The New Yorker*;
Adrienne Gordon; Duncan Chapman; Anthony Weller; Thomas Sanchez; Nelson Ramos; Karl Francis;
Giorgio Arcangeletti; Christopher Hunt; Katya Slavenska; Gail Gordon; Molly Gleason; Winston
Conrad; Andrei Glasberg; Steve Worthington; Howard Junker; Nancy Jarvis and Steve Farrand;
Barnaby Conrad, Jr.; Jeannette Etheridge of Tosca Café; Morton's of Chicago; Mark Miller; Doug
Biederbeck; Rafe de la Guerroniere; Bill Getty, Gavin Newsom, and Kelly Phleger of Plump Jack.
Special thanks to Rick Bolen for his photography and friendship.

Page 2: *John Colao,* Triumvir I, (Bolivar Lonsdale, Montecristo No. 2, Cohiba Robusto), *1995, archival
toned silver gelatin, 14 x 11 inches. (Modernism Gallery, San Francisco)*
Page 3: *Orson Welles (UPI/Bettmann)*
Page 5: *Winston Churchill (Bettmann Archive)*
Page 6: *Guy Diehl,* Punch at the Stork, *1996, detail, acrylic on canvas, 16 x 19 inches (Modernism Gallery, San
Francisco)*

CONTENTS

A Very Smoky Introduction

"If I cannot smoke in heaven, then I shall not go."

MARK TWAIN

Queen Victoria was a virulent anti-tobacco lobbyist, and when she died in 1901 her son and heir, Edward VII, who was an avid cigar smoker, gathered his intimate friends at Buckingham Palace. The men were waiting in a large drawing room when the new king entered with a lit cigar in hand. "Gentleman," he proclaimed, "you may smoke."

Edward was among the many enthusiasts enthralled by the cigar's charm. Mention the word *cigar* and seductive images swirl across the mind—an Edwardian banquet where every man has a moustache, a crown of laurel leaves, and a burning cigar; a late afternoon at the racetrack; a floor show at the Tropicana in Havana; a stroll through Manhattan's Little Italy with a man named Don Vito; any photograph of Winston Churchill; an Aston Martin careening out of the London fog; a quiet smoke on horseback in the Rocky Mountains; the German baroness in Gstaad who says, "I vant to puff it, too"; the birth of a child; golfing in the rain at St. Andrews and a companionable smoke with Fergus, the caddy; another bottle of Chateau Lafite 1959 opened after midnight.

Edouard Manet's portrait of Stéphane Mallarmé (detail) depicts the poet caught in a reverie of smoke. (Musée d'Orsay, Paris)

The cigar is an organic object, a high bourgeois art form, an international commodity, and a mythic signifier loaded with so many dimensions

that we can never understand, love, or defend them all. Think of the grandiloquent gestures that have come down to us with the cigar! At the Battle of Königgratz, Bismarck walked through the human carnage, intent on smoking his last cigar, but seeing a mortally wounded dragoon, he lit the cigar and put it in the poor man's lips; Napoleon's Marshall Ney, about to be executed by troops under his own command, requested a last smoke, a gesture that is now universally accepted as condemned man's right; the Italian statesman Mazzini offered cigars to the men who had come to assassinate him, which so moved the villains they fell to their knees to receive his pardon; and Alfred

Lord Tennyson, while visiting Venice, dismissed its charm because "they had no good cigars there, my lord; and I left the place in disgust."

Cigars have played a signature role in the private and public lives of many great men. One cannot remember Winston Churchill without a fine—and usually mammoth—Cuban cigar protruding from his mouth. Ulysses S. Grant smoked through every battle of the Civil War. Sigmund Freud attributed his emotional and physical well-being to the fifteen cigars he smoked each day. Einstein daydreamed about energy, mass, and time over cigar ash. Literature owes a debt to Mark Twain's and Rudyard Kipling's cigars. Women, too, have enjoyed the products of Havana. Early feminist George Sand said, "The cigar is the perfect complement to an elegant lifestyle," while her lover Alfred de Musset, once told a colleague, "Any cigar smoker is a friend, because I know how he feels."

Cigars are smoked in nearly every country in the world, but tobacco—and tobacco smoking—came from the New World. Columbus found the Caribbean natives smoking it in 1492. When Cortez marched into Montezuma's court, he was fascinated by the Aztec priests who used smoking rituals to communicate with the supernatural. Early European explorers returned to smoke in the princely palaces of Spain and Portugal, and tobacco symbolized the wealth of the Americas.

Nineteenth-century Europe spawned the first golden age of cigars. The legendary cigarmakers of Sevilla were a well-kept secret until Napoleon's campaigns in Spain. Within a short time "seegars," as they were first known, were the rage of London and Paris. Composer Franz Liszt, who never traveled without a stack of double-walled cedar boxes filled with cigars, once rhapsodized that "A good Cuban cigar closes the door to the vulgarities of the world." When he entered a monastery at the end

After Queen Victoria's death, the English King Edward VII uttered those felicitous words, "Gentlemen, you may smoke." (Library of Congress)

Composer Franz Liszt once rhapsodized that "A good Cuban cigar closes the door to the vulgarities of the world." (Bettmann Archive)

of his life, Liszt beseeched the Father Superior to allow him to smoke. The cleric granted this, perhaps believing that an earthly pleasure sometimes leads to heavenly enlightenment.

Cartoonists depict genius at work with a lightbulb glowing above the head, but I think great insights are better symbolized by a plume of cigar smoke. In the twentieth century, cigar smoke wreathed Thomas Edison in Menlo Park, Sigmund Freud in Vienna, and General Douglas MacArthur in the Pacific Campaign. The blue cloud hovered over Ira Gershwin, Orson Welles, and H. L. Mencken. Charlie Chaplin smoked it up as the tramp in *The Gold Rush*, and Hollywood stars such as W. C. Fields, Groucho Marx, Jack Benny, and Edward G. Robinson often puffed away on the big screen.

The novelist Italo Calvino felt that the cigar embodied no less than "the eternal attributes of prestige, success, and *savoir faire*." During most of its history the cigar has long been a well-known player in the world of kings, statesmen, politicians, financiers, tycoons, and the underworld. To some critics, however, cigars connote unchecked power, overweening egos, a cult of greed, and shady

Opposite: Groucho Marx as Professor Quincy Adams Wagstaff with Robert Greig in the 1932 Paramount film Horsefeathers *(Culver Pictures).*

deals done in the back room. How unfair, I say. True lovers of the leaf view the cigar not only as nirvana for the taste buds, but as a skeleton key to camaraderie, shared joy, passionate intellect, and bountiful goodwill. Cigars have been ritual accessories for males gathered before and after military battles, business deals, poker games, bar mitzvahs, stag parties, and weddings. The boss used to hand an employee a cigar along with a promotion. How different was the world in which our fathers and grandfathers came of age!

Our age is an era of doubt, a world divided into cringing smokers and finger-shaking non-smokers. We know cigarette smoking in unmoderated amounts is hostile

OUTLINES
OF
ANATOMY
WARELL

to your health. Yet cigar smoking—in *moderation*—is certifiably beneficial to relieving stress. (A growing number of doctors and insurance companies recognize this.) "Cigarettes are for chain-smoking, cigars must be smoked one at a time, peaceably, with all the leisure in the world." says Cuban-born novelist G. Cabrera Infante. "Cigarettes are of the instant, cigars are for eternity."

FROM THE INVISIBLE MAN

by H.G. Wells (1897)

(UPI/Bettmann)

After he had done eating, and he made a heavy meal, the Invisible Man demanded a cigar. He bit the end savagely before Kemp could find a knife, and cursed when the outer leaf loosened. It was strange to see him smoking; his mouth, and throat, pharynx and nares, became visible as a sort of whirling smoke cast.

"This blessed gift of smoking!" he said, and puffed vigorously. "I'm lucky to have fallen upon you, Kemp. You must help me. Fancy tumbling on you just now! I'm in a devilish scrape. I've been mad, I think. The things I have been through! But we will do things yet. Let me tell you—"

He helped himself to more whiskey and soda. Kemp got up, looked about him, and fetched himself a glass from his spare room. "It's wild—but I suppose I may drink."

"You haven't changed much, Kemp, these dozen years. You fair men don't. Cool and methodical—after the first collapse. I must tell you. We will work together!"

"But how was it all done?" said Kemp, "and how did you get like this?"

"For God's sake, let me smoke in peace for a little while! And then I will begin to tell you."

But the story was not told that night. The Invisible Man's wrist was growing painful, he was feverish, exhausted, and his mind came round to brood upon his chase down the hill and the struggle about the inn. He spoke in fragments of Marvel, he smoked faster, his voice grew angry. Kemp tried to gather what he could.

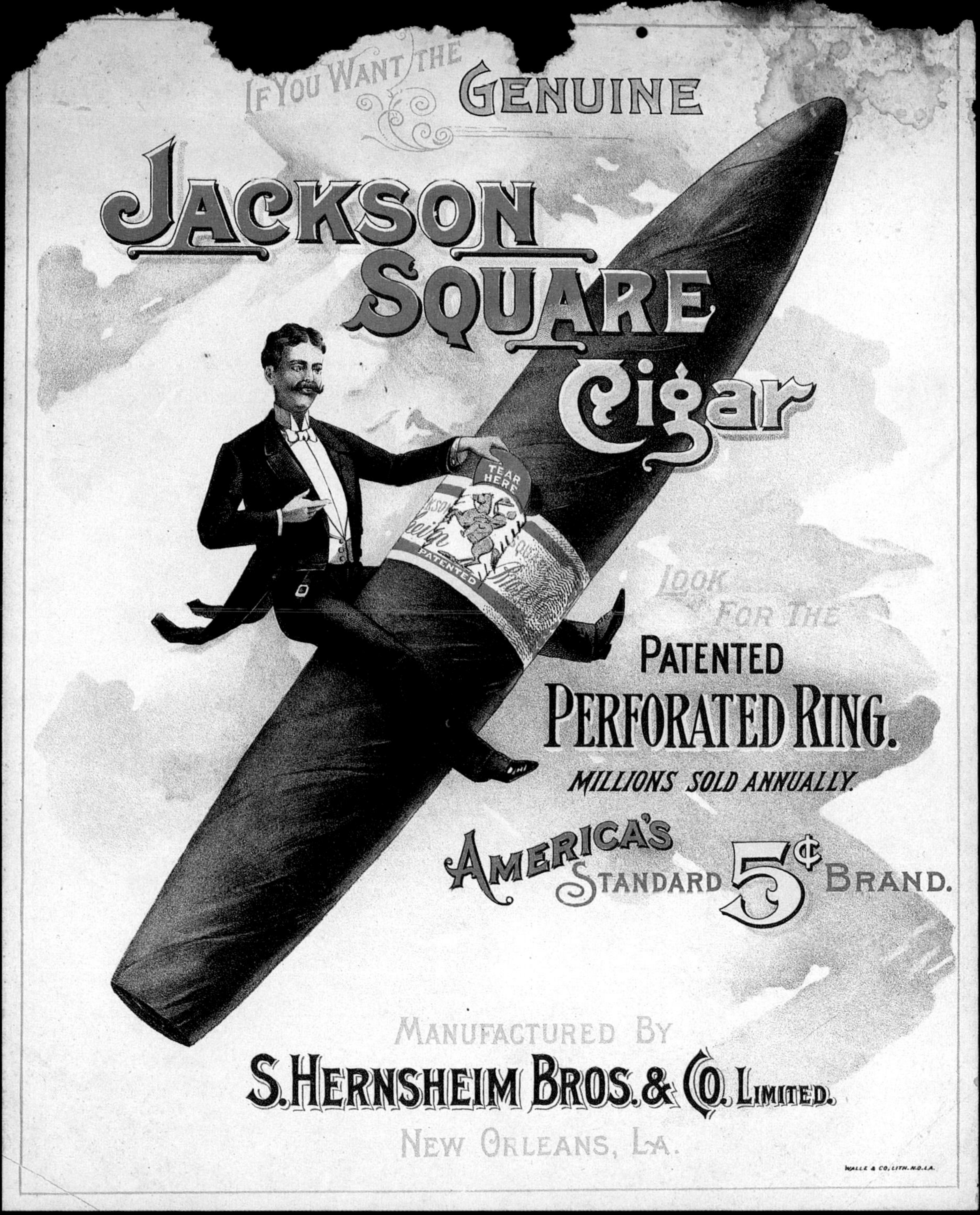

IF YOU WANT THE GENUINE
JACKSON SQUARE Cigar
TEAR HERE
PATENTED
LOOK FOR THE
PATENTED
PERFORATED RING.
MILLIONS SOLD ANNUALLY.
AMERICA'S STANDARD 5¢ BRAND.
MANUFACTURED BY
S. HERNSHEIM BROS. & CO. LIMITED.
NEW ORLEANS, LA.
WALLE & CO, LITH. N.O. LA.

In 1964, the year the Surgeon General issued the watershed report on health and smoking, Americans consumed nine billion (mostly machine-made) cigars. By 1992, U.S. consumption had dropped to two billion per year. Yet today, the world is experiencing a cigar renaissance. In 1992, Marvin Shanken, publisher of *The Wine Spectator*, launched *Cigar Aficionado*, an over-sized glossy magazine. "There was no budget," wrote Shanken in the second year. "There weren't even any expectations." The magazine's readership zoomed from 40,000 the first year to its current 250,000—and it is still rising like a smoke signal from happy hedonists. (A rival, *Smoke*, made its debut in late 1995, the same year a movie called *Smoke* became a cult hit, and a thoroughbred named "Cigar" became the racehorse of the year.)

Cigar Aficionado, one of the most successful magazine start-ups of this decade, has rallied the cigar industry and created a forum for cigar smokers all over the world. American cigar merchants from Madison Avenue to Rodeo Drive have noted a resurgence of interest among young men and women. Similar reports come in from London and Paris.

According to U.S. government statistics, only 99 million cigars were imported in 1992. Suddenly, imports to America rose to 109 million cigars in 1993, passed to 125 million in 1994, and hit 174 million in 1995. The estimate for 1996 is over 200 million. Not included in these figures are the approximately six million illegal Cuban cigars that are

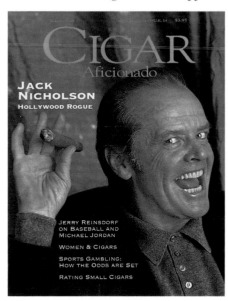 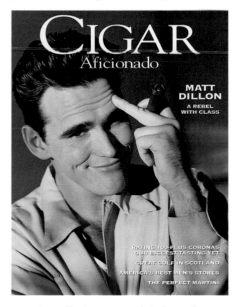

Jack Nicholson (far left) took up cigar smoking to break a cigarette habit. Film star Matt Dillon (left) appeared on the cover of Cigar Aficionado *in 1996.*

purchased abroad and smuggled into the country (usually in a genteel fashion for private consumption). New cigar labels and shops appear every month. Yuppies fight to get invited to black tie cigar banquets at hotels and restaurants. Cigar bars and private smoking clubs are springing up from Manhattan to Los Angeles. There are over two dozen cigar web-sites on the Internet, vintage cigars sell for thousands of dollars at auction, while travel companies offer special cigar-smoking cruises to the Caribbean.

BOOTH

The resurgence seems a direct response to modern civilization, where telephones, e-mail, and traffic jams have carved the day—that is, your very life—into a series of nerve-wracking, dehumanizing chores. As San Francisco financier Steve Worthington told me, "A hand-made cigar is a rebellion against frenzy and insanity; it means sup-porting contemplation over rash impulse, and represents a civilized revolution."

The cigar is both primitive and civilized. It is the urban man's camp fire, a bright cheery glow in a dark, increasingly uncivil world.

The book you are holding grew out of my own love of cigars and cigar lore, and is dedicated to the poetic, historical, and artistic aspects of this wonderful, timeless pastime.

CHAPTER ONE

EARLY HISTORY

*The Indians used a Y-shaped tube, putting the two ends of
the fork up their nostrils and the tube in the burning grasses.*

FERNANDEZ DE OVIEDO, *HISTORY AND NATURAL HISTORY OF THE WEST INDIES*, 1535

*Christopher Columbus not only
discovered the New World but
was astounded to find its native
inhabitants smoking prototypes of
the cigar. (Library of Congress)*

The cigar's history begins with the arrival of Christopher Columbus on the island of San Salvador, and his subsequent exploration of the large island called Cuba, which he reached on October 28, 1492. That day the discoverer noted in his log that his colleagues met many male and female "Indians" who carried "a little lighted brand made from a kind of plant whose aroma it was their custom to inhale."

One of his lieutenants, Luis de Torrès, a translator of Hebrew, Chaldean, and Arabic, observed that the natives carried "a lighted piece of coal and some grasses, and inhale the aroma using catapults which in their language they call *tabacos*." The catapult may have been a tube-shaped construction of plant leaves filled with tobacco. Columbus himself observed that these aboriginal Cubans called the plant *cohiba*, a word that has survived 500 years to become the brand name *Cohiba*, one of the preeminent cigars in Castro's Cuba. Historians emphasize the role of Rodriguo de Xeres, a fellow explorer who was the first to smoke a cigar—or whatever it was—and subsequently did so every day of the exploration.

This early engraving shows New World men picking tobacco leaves and stuffing them into tubes made of hardier leaves, perhaps palm. Europeans had never seen any type of smoking before. (Musée de la Seita, Paris)

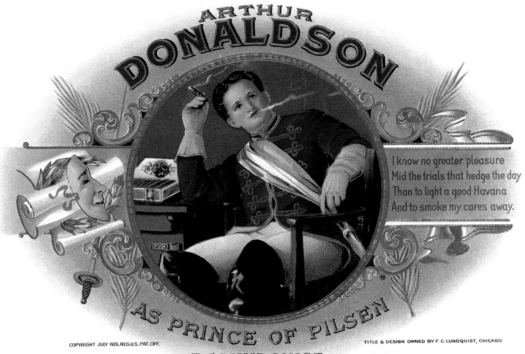

ARTHUR DONALDSON

AS PRINCE OF PILSEN

I know no greater pleasure
Mid the trials that hedge the day
Than to light a good Havana
And to smoke my cares away.

COPYRIGHT JULY 1926, REG.U.S.PAT.OFF.   TITLE & DESIGN OWNED BY F. C. LUNDQUIST, CHICAGO

MAKER F.C.LUNDQUIST CHICAGO.

Columbus returned three more times to the New World in the next 22 years—an incredible feat in that era—and explored the tobacco lands of San Salvador, Cuba, Guadalupe, Puerto Rico, Jamaica, Venezuela, Columbia, Honduras, and the island of Hispaniola, which later became the Dominican Republic and Haiti. Other explorers such as Amerigo Vespucci, Alvarez Pedro Cabral, and Ferdinand Magellan also encountered tobacco first hand. Some Spanish histories say Cortez was the first to bring tobacco back to Europe in 1518; others credit Francisco Hernandez Gonçalo as late as 1570. Portuguese experts say it was Hernandez de Toledo in 1520, who brought leaves harvested in the Tobasco

Opposite: A wooden cigar store Indian, circa 1895 (Bettmann Archive)

province of the Yucatan back to Lisbon. The Dutch claim it was Damien de Goes, who brought the seed from Florida and presented it to King Sebastian of Portugal.

The origin of the word *cigar* has been linked falsely to the Spanish word *cigaral* (cicada). In fact, it comes from the ancient Mayans. The *Popol Vuh*, a chronicle of the Quiché tribe, gives the cigar a name pronounced *Jiq* or *Ciq*. The Spanish *cigarro* is derived from the Maya word *Ciq-Sigan*. Actually, the word floated and danced in oral and written tradition

RSITY
GAR
RIUM
LITTLE CIGARS
Loveras cut to
Bengals
Robert Burns
Telonette
Buffo
Imperialette
ALL KINDS
HOME MADE
FRES
PURE COFF
OVR
BISMARK
PICKLED
ROLLED
SWISS CHEESE
CREAM
TONGUE
PURE
ICE COL
Y

for two centuries until it appeared as *cigale* in the writings of Father Labat (1700) and as *seegar* in the *New English Dictionary* of 1735. The noble cigar store Indian, then, is a very real and appropriate symbol for tobacco.

The French Ambassador to Lisbon, Jean Nicot, was such an enthusiast that the tobacco plant *Nicotiana Tabacum* was named for him. He gave it to Catherine de Medici in France, who claimed it had medicinal value. By the late sixteenth century, sensualists in Spain, Portugal, Italy, and England were familiar with tobacco.

While tobacco recruited enthusiasts in the Old World, it also inspired enemies.

THE DUC DE LA ROCHEFOUCAULD-LIANCOURT

he Duc de la Rochefoucauld-Liancourt is the author of one of the oldest known celebrations of the cigar. Sent to America in 1794 on a special mission to present a message from the French revolutionary government, the Duke wrote this about his sea voyage:

"The cigar is a great resource. It is necessary to have traveled for a long time on a ship to understand that at least the cigar affords you the pleasure of smoking. It raises your spirits. Are you troubled by something? The cigar dissolves it. Are you subject to aches and pains (or bad temper)? The cigar will change your disposition. Are you harassed by unpleasant thoughts? Smoking a cigar puts one in a frame of mind to dispense with these. Do you ever feel a little faint from hunger? A cigar satisfies the yearning. If you are obsessed by sad thoughts, a cigar will take your mind off of them. Finally don't you sometimes have some pleasant remembrance or consoling thought? A cigar will reinforce this. Sometimes they die out, and happy are those who do not need to relight too quickly. I hardly need to say anything more about the cigar, to which I dedicate this little eulogy for past services rendered."

(Bettmann Archive)

Larry Rivers, Dutch Masters and Cigars I, *1964, oil on canvas and mixed media, 96 x 67 ¹/₂ inches. (Collection of Jacques Kaplan/Courtesy Marlborough Gallery, New York)*

Nº 167 Sevilla   Faª de Tabacos. Elaboracion de Cigarros   E. Beauchy

Based on the opinion of his doctors, the English king, James I, denounced it in 1619 as "stinking grass," and disapproved of a fashion "which was imitating the beastly manners of those godless and slavish Indians." Other monarchs, who had previously encouraged importation, echoed his sentiments. Pope Urban VIII forbade Spanish priests to smoke cigars. Sultan Ahmed hacked off the noses of any subjects found smoking a cigar. Russian Czar Michael Fedorivich III, the Persian Shah Abbas I, and the Ottoman sultan Murad IV, all took sides against tobacco. The great fire of Moscow in 1650 was conveniently blamed on a smoker. In France, Cardinal Richelieu laid a heavy tax on tobacco.

From the start, the Spanish were the prime architects of the cigar industry. By the early 1800s, the royal cigar factories of Sevilla were experiencing astounding growth. It is important to note that no one in South or Central America had made a cigar as we know it today—that credit goes to the Spaniards. Prior to that time, New World natives had wrapped tobacco in leaves of other plants like palm or maize. In 1831 King Ferdinand VII granted Cubans the

Nicotiana inserta infundibulo ex quo hauriunt fumum Indi & nautcleri.

Above: The rare American label Old Sport was printed in New York City. (Collection Wayne H. Dunn, Mission Viejo, California)

Left: The royal cigar factories of Sevilla became world famous. (Culver Pictures)

---

right to produce and sell tobacco in their homeland. The island soon swarmed with producers who were the exclusive makers for the Spanish Crown. This tradition continues even under Fidel Castro, who every year sends a symbolic batch of the best cigars—in recent years Cohibas and Trinidads—to the Spanish king Juan Carlos. To this day Spain remains the world's largest importer of Cuban cigars—and offers them to its people at the lowest prices.

Tobacco was cultivated widely in the British colonies of North America, but at first the crops were intended for pipe smokers. In 1762 Israel Putnam returned to Connecticut from active duty with the British army in Cuba bearing a large supply of cigars and introduced the miracle to Connecticut. Putnam was a hero at the Battle of Bunker Hill and went on to become a Revolutionary War general. Following the war, factories for cigars sprang up in Connecticut, Pennsylvania, and New York. The word *stogie* comes

Israel Putnam was a Revolutionary War hero who promoted the tobacco industry in Connecticut. (Corbis/Bettmann)

from Conestoga, Pennsylvania, which had cigar factories (and later produced the famed covered wagons that carried American settlers westward).

English veterans of the 1814 campaign against Napoleonic forces in Spain brought the cigar to England, while French troops introduced it to Paris. In 1823 only fifteen thousand cigars were imported into Britain; by 1840 that figure jumped to 13 million. Popular among the bourgeoisie, they were also favored by Lord Byron, Victor Hugo, and Charles Baudelaire, as well as composers Georges Bizet and Maurice Ravel. During the 1880s, London financier Leopold de Rothschild instructed the Hoyo de Monterrey factory in Havana to make a short cigar with a large ring size so that he could enjoy full flavor in a short time.

Paul Garmirian notes in his book *The Gourmet Guide to Cigars* that English consumption of imported cigars remained low because the cigars were heavily taxed as a luxury item, whereas pipe tobacco was not. Domestically made English cigars—even though constructed with imported tobacco—were taxed less heavily.

Despite the tariff, Spanish cigars—known as Sevilles—were popular in London and Paris, where the post-prandial cigar became a tradition. Smoking rooms called "divans" sprang up in

David Bates, Man with Cigar, 1986-7, painted bronze, 16 x 12 ³/₄ x 7 inches, Edition of 6. (John Berggruen Gallery, San Francisco)

London, while British and European railroads introduced smoking cars. Silk smoking jackets came into vogue, allowing gentlemen to bask in smoke and ash without stinking up their fine clothes; the smoking jacket evolved into the tuxedo, which to this day the French refer to as *le smoking*. (France remains one of the most cigar-friendly countries in the world.)

Cigar smoking in America rose dramatically after the Civil War with many U.S. companies producing cigars made of domestic wrappers and Havana filler. Cigars and Cuban-American politics have long been mixed. From 1881 to 1895, the Cuban writer and revolutionary José Martí lived in New York City. When he finally returned to liberate Cuba from Spanish rule, he had the support of thousands of Cuban cigar makers who had fled to Key West and Tampa. The plans for the rebellion were sent from Key West to Havana rolled in a cigar. This first revolution—with the morale-building presence of Teddy Roosevelt and American forces at San Juan Hill—was successful, although it caused the death of Martí, who today is considered the Cuban equivalent of George Washington. (Sixty years later in 1955, Castro's supporters delivered messages hidden in cigars to Fidel in his Cuban prison cell on the Isle of Pines.)

CHAPTER TWO

POLITICS, POWER, AND THE CIGAR

"What this country really needs is a good five-cent cigar."

THOMAS RILEY MARSHALL, U.S. VICE PRESIDENT, 1920

Winston Churchill was honored with a cigar label El Ministro (the Minister).

The most famous cigar-smoking politician was also the greatest man of our century: Winston Churchill. He discovered cigars at the age of 22, while garrisoned in Havana, Cuba, in 1895. They became a life-long passion. By most estimates he smoked at least ten cigars per day—or roughly 3,000 per year, which works out to over a quarter million in his lifetime. During the Second World War, Cuban cigar companies sent 5,000 cigars each year to keep him well-stocked against shipping interruptions caused by German U-boats. Although Sir Winston smoked many kinds of cigars, his favorite was a seven-incher with a 48 ring gauge. The Romeo y Julieta factory in Havana immortalized that size by naming it the Churchill.

Once during the war, Churchill was required to take his first high-altitude airplane flight in an unpressurized cabin. According to his renowned biographer Martin Gilbert, when the prime minister went to the airfield the day before to be outfitted with a flight suit and oxygen mask, he requested a special mask designed to accommodate his cigar smoking; the

Winston Churchill toured England by train in July of 1941, his cigar ever present. Churchill smoked at least ten cigars a day, which adds up to nearly a quarter of a million over his lifetime. (Library of Congress)

next day he was puffing away 15,000 feet above the earth.

In her 1941 memoir, *I Was Winston Churchill's Private Secretary*, Phyllis Moir wrote that "Mr. Churchill's cigar has taken the place of Chamberlain's umbrella as Britain's national emblem. The pottery works of Stoke-on-Trent are turning out for the American market Toby jugs fashioned into the likeness of the Prime Minister, a cigar clenched between his teeth in such a way as to give him

Opposite: During the 1941 London Blitz, German bombs destroyed Alfred Dunhill's famous shop in Duke Street. After inspecting the damage, Alfred H. Dunhill telephoned Winston Churchill at 2 A.M. to inform him, "Your cigars are safe, sir." Dunhill himself showed British resolve by personally manning a makeshift desk to assure clients he was still in business. (Courtesy Alfred Dunhill, London)

a particularly pugnacious expression. When King George and Queen Elizabeth visited the pottery works the King examined the Toby jugs with critical interest. 'I do not think he smokes his cigars at such a low angle,' the King remarked earnestly, thereby sending the pottery firm's executives into a hurried conference on the slant of Winston Churchill's cigars."

After Churchill steered Britain through its "darkest hours," there was a proposal to build a gigantic statue of the statesman with cigar in hand on the Cliffs of Dover; his glowing cigar ash was to be a revolving lighthouse beacon for ships at sea. Though this monument was never built, England is populated with smaller statues of Churchill, and he appears in a stained glass window in the parish church at Cransley. The cigar, of course, is ever present.

The public was well aware of Churchill's cigar passion, and went so far as to use it against him. During the electoral campaign of June 1945, Labor party opponents criticized him for smoking expensive cigars while the common folk endured the rationing of

HENDRICKS.—Ah, Governor, the CAPADURA is a good representative of our party. It is an honest Cigar. IT GIVES VALUE FOR THE MONEY.

CLEVELAND.—Right you are, Senator! Only keep the boys well supplied with them, as I did, and New York is good for another 200,000 majority.

Ohio's Senator Thomas A. Henricks and President Grover Cleveland smoking in a cartoon of the 1880s. (Culver Pictures)

cigarettes. In 1947, a Labor member of the House of Lords, Lord Chorley, suggested that Churchill be deprived of cigars for two years as punishment for his attacks on Labor leaders. Though Labor held the majority, when put to a vote the proposal was defeated.

Churchill shared his passion, and regularly sent cigars to his friend Sibelius, the great Finnish composer, who also lived into his eighties. When guests such as Charlie Chaplin and Albert Einstein visited Sir Winston at his home, Chartwell Manor, the statesman welcomed them with a long cordial dinner followed by his best cigars.

Phyllis Moir recalled that Churchill always traveled with several boxes of long, very strong-smelling, and very expensive Havana cigars. "He smoked about fifteen of them a day but seldom smoked one to the end. He threw them away after he had got the best out of them. I very rarely saw him without one. Hostesses invariably complained that wherever he went he left behind him a trail of cigar ash on their valuable carpets." When reading in bed he was apt to let his ash fall and burn holes in his silk pajamas. He kept a candle burning by the bed for relighting cigars.

Phyllis Moir boasted of Churchill's health in spite of his high intake of champagne, brandy, and cigars. "He is blessed with a positively Herculean constitution. In spite of the terrific pace at which he has lived he can proudly state that now in his sixties he is in excellent physical condition. His blood pressure is practically normal. For some strange reason he rather enjoys having it taken. This is one of his few little foibles."

Viscount Montgomery (the wartime general known as "Monty") once boasted, "I do not drink. I do not smoke. I sleep a great deal. That is why I am in one-hundred-per-cent form."

Churchill, who found Monty's vanity often hard to accept, retorted, "I drink a great deal. I sleep little, and I smoke cigar after cigar. That is why I am in *two*-hundred-per-cent form." And he lived to the age of 90.

Cigars in the White House have been a tradition for almost two centuries. Nineteen of the 41 presidents have smoked "seegars." George Washington raised tobacco as a cash crop at Mount Vernon, but there is no evidence that he smoked a cigar. John Adams, our second president, fancied a fine cigar, as did his son John Quincy Adams, our sixth president. The first president to smoke in the newly built White House was James Madison, the country's fourth president, who smoked avidly until his demise in 1836 at the age of 85. (His wife Dolley openly pinched snuff.)

Andrew Jackson and his much-maligned wife smoked cigars together. Zachary Taylor, a hero of the Mexican War who was elected in 1848, had to smoke alone or

John Adams and his son John Quincy Adams (pictured here) were early American presidents who smoked cigars. (Library of Congress)

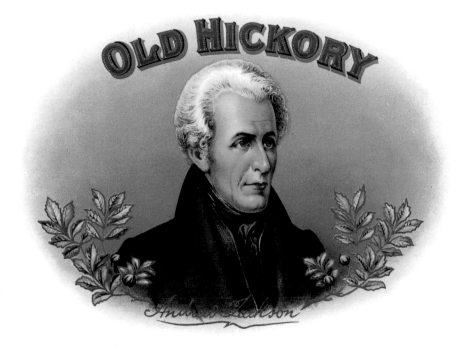

President Andrew Jackson, known as Old Hickory, smoked cigars with his wife in the White House.

An "OLD SOLDIER," left by GEN U. S. GRANT, at
HOUSEWORTH'S PHOTOGRAPHIC STUDIO,
12 MONTGOMERY STREET, -   -   -   -   - SAN FRANCISCO, CAL.

with male friends because his wife complained that cigars made her ill. Among the men who enjoyed a smoke with Jackson was his son-in-law Jefferson Davis, who later became president of the Confederacy during the Civil War.

On the opposite side of the battle lines was General Ulysses S. Grant, who was known for smoking ten cigars per day. His habit increased after the battle of Fort Donelson in the winter of 1862. Grant had been a light smoker previously, but newspaper accounts reported that he was smoking in the midst of battle, and many people

Opposite: Cigar of Ulysses S. Grant. (California Historical Society)

began sending him boxes of cigars as a gesture of support. "As many as ten thousand were soon received," he recalled. "I gave away all that I could get rid of, but having such a quantity on hand I naturally smoked more than I would have done under ordinary circumstances, and I have continued the habit ever since."

THE CALVERT LITH CO.DETROIT.

This rare cigar label depicting Civil War opponents Robert E. Lee and Ulysses S. Grant as Fellow Citizens symbolized the hopes for peace after the struggle that nearly tore apart the nation.

The Civil War was a cigar war, whereas all the wars of the twentieth century were cigarette wars. I am thinking of a scene from Stephen Crane's *The Red Badge of Courage*: "As the horseman wheeled his animal and galloped away he turned to shout over his shoulder, 'Don't forget that box of cigars!' The colonel mumbled a reply. The youth wondered what a box of cigars had to do with war." Actually, quite a bit—at Antietam General Robert E. Lee delivered orders wrapped around three cigars.

By the time Grant ran for president on the Republican ticket, the cigar had become such a well-known aspect of his persona that the 1868 campaign song was "A Smokin'

His Cigar." The Democrats had a retort, singing, "I smoke my weed and drink my gin, playing with the people's tin." (Grant did, in fact, die of throat cancer.)

After Grant, it was the rare American president who didn't smoke a cigar. Chester Arthur, our 21st president, was a *bon vivant* who enjoyed champagne and cigars after a

Woodrow Wilson's vice president, Thomas R. Marshall, held a cigar as he threw out the first ball for the baseball season. He uttered the immortal line: "What this country really needs is a good five-cent cigar." (Library of Congress)

repast. Benjamin Harrison had cigars shipped to him from his hometown of Indianapolis. William McKinley, the 25th president, wouldn't smoke in public, but loved to have one privately. White House Chief Usher Ike Hoover recalled that "McKinley had a passion for cigars and was perhaps the most intense smoker of all the presidents during my life. One never saw him without a cigar in his mouth except at meals or when asleep." When he was with male colleagues, McKinley smoked his Garcias; when he was in the company of his wife, who didn't like smoke, he broke his cigar in half and sucked on it.

At 300 pounds William Howard Taft was surely the most oval man to occupy the Oval Office. He began as a cigar smoker but forsook them near the end of his term. Teddy Roosevelt didn't smoke, nor did Woodrow Wilson, but Wilson's otherwise forgotten vice president, Thomas R. Marshall, made cigar history. After listening with disgust to a rival politician rambling on for hours in the Senate about "what America needs most" the vice president harpooned the blowhard with an immortal line: "What

Unknown artist, I'm always glad when you light a Cremo Perfecto, *c. 1935, offset lithograph,*

40 x 35 inches. (Modernism Gallery, San Francisco)

America really needs is a good five-cent cigar." Unfortunately, he got only part of his wish; as America turned away from the fine art of handrolling and machines took over, the price became cheap, but the product lackluster.

Warren Harding, Calvin Coolidge, and Herbert Hoover carried on the White House tradition. Dubbed "Silent Cal" in the press, Coolidge believed in talking softly and carrying a big cigar. When people offered him a cigar, he would examine theirs carefully for size and aroma, then one-up them by producing an enormous 12-inch super corona from his own vest pocket—*now that's a cigar!* Coolidge made a practice of inviting congressmen (whose legislative support he needed) for 8 AM. breakfasts; not until cigars were passed around did the dickering get serious.

Kennedy recruited his press secretary, Pierre Salinger, to round up 1,100 cigars before signing the document commanding the 1963 embargo against Cuba. (UPI/Bettmann) Right: Alabama Governor George Wallace smoked a cigar in 1972 while listening to Vice President Spiro T. Agnew addressing the National Governor's Conference. (UPI/Bettmann)

Franklin D. Roosevelt and Dwight D. Eisenhower smoked cigarettes, as did their wives, but their guests were graciously offered cigars. While stomping the bone-dry Texas Panhandle for votes, FDR's vice president, John Nance Garner, humidified his cigars by putting them inside his sweaty Stetson.

John Kennedy, the last president to regularly light up, acquired the taste as a young man, encouraged by his father Joe Kennedy, a financial heavyweight and FDR's ambassador to the Court of St. James. Kennedy usually smoked the petit corona size.

One day in 1961, shortly after the failed Bay of Pigs invasion, the president took legendary action that has become a

classic anecdote of cigar lore. JFK called his cigar-smoking press secretary Pierre Salinger into the Oval Office and said, "I need a lot of cigars."

"How many, Mr. President?"

"About a thousand. Tomorrow morning, call all your friends who have cigars and just get as many as you can."

Salinger rushed out and grabbed as many H. Upmann petits as he could find. The next morning there was an urgent message for him to enter the Oval Office immediately. "How did you do on the cigars last night?" asked Kennedy.

"Mr. President," replied Salinger, "I was very successful. I got eleven hundred."

With that, Kennedy opened a drawer in his desk and pulled out a decree banning all Cuban products from entry into the United States.

"Good," he replied. "Now that I have enough cigars to last awhile, I can sign this!"

After JFK's death, his widow gave Salinger a memento that he keeps with him always: the president's cigar case engraved with those famous initials. Unfortunately, the embargo is still in place against Cuba.

Above: Pierre Salinger, press secretary to President Kennedy, in 1961. (UPI/ Bettmann)

Richard Nixon wasn't an enthusiastic cigar smoker, but he understood the diplomatic benefits of the convivial ritual. He was the last president to offer cigars after dinner to men gathered in the Green Room. Jimmy Carter didn't smoke. Gerald Ford favored a pipe. Ronald Reagan eschewed tobacco, but resisted pressure from his doctor to ban smok-

Opposite: Silver and crystal ashtray, silver cigar tube, and fine cigars by Davidoff of Geneva. (Photo by Rick Bolen) Below: Conservative radio host Rush Limbaugh appeared on the cover of Cigar Aficionado in 1994.

ing in the White House because he felt that it would be ungracious to guests. Under the Bush Administration, tobacco products were not offered to guests, but ashtrays were still visible in state rooms. Bill Clinton has been photographed smoking cigars on the golf course, but Hillary Rodham Clinton recently banned all smoking inside 1600 Pennyslvania Avenue. There have been rumors of cigar smoking on the balconies, however. On the Supreme Court, Justices Clarence Thomas and Antonin Scalia smoke cigars.

Should the cigar, symbol of civility, be drafted into partisan politics? A letter from *Cigar Aficionado* (Winter 1994) reader Kevin Grinstead of St. Louis, Missouri, registered dismay that some readers had actually canceled their subscriptions after the magazine put right-wing radio commentator Rush Limbaugh on the cover. "If these people are truly cigar lovers, surely they can understand the huge influence Rush has had on the cigar-smoking industry as well as subscriptions to your magazine."

Mr. Grinstead went on to say, "If anything, a case could be made that cigar smoking pulls together people of different ideologies. What do Rush the Conservative, Clinton the Liberal, and Castro the Dictator all have in common? Of course, they all love

President Clinton enjoyed a cigar on February 27, 1996, at the Belle Haven Country Club in Alexandria, Virginia. He's no longer allowed to smoke in the White House. (AP/Mark Wilson/Wide World Photos)

cigars. I think this is common ground to start a meaningful dialogue. Let's get Rush, Castro, and Clinton together in a neutral site—say a raft adrift off the coast of Florida. Buy a few Dominican or Honduran cigars. Invite Cosby and Letterman to help break the ice and see what develops. Maybe they could end the Cuban embargo."

American business and cigars have long been linked. J. P. Morgan owned a diamond-encrusted cigar cutter in the form of a golden dog; when the tail was raised, it opened its mouth. The Mexican company Te-Amo makes an eight-and-one-half-inch cigar called The CEO. In the 1987 movie *Wall Street*, Charlie Sheen plays an

FROM THE
CONNOISSEUR'S BOOK
by Zino Davidoff (1969)

Vladimir Lenin (Library of Congress)

In the beginning, I smoked like a glutton. My parents were cigar merchants in Kiev. My father's store was a small one and all the family made cigarettes by hand, cigarettes with blond tobacco imported from Turkey. This store was not like any other. From time to time, bizarre gentlemen with conspiratorial looks would gather there. They *were* conspirators. And just as the liberator of Cuba, José Martí, exiled in Florida, used to send messages rolled in cigars, so the enemies of the Czars in Kiev carried out their plans behind a cigar-smoke screen. Eventually the conspiratorial ring was discovered and I, with my family, left Russia in a covered wagon. In Geneva my father opened a small workshop and began again to build up a trade. Other exiles came to the shop. They were feverishly preparing for the revolution. One of them greatly impressed me. He had a thin face, brilliant eyes, and spoke in a loud voice. He also took cigars and didn't pay for them. My father never tried to recover the money. On a bill which I have kept as a souvenir are stamped the words *Not Paid* and the name of this customer—Vladimir Ulyanov. Not until later was he known as Lenin.

ambitious stockbroker who gets the attention of corporate raider Gordon Gekko by presenting him with a box of Cuban cigars.

Until recent times, cigar smoke wafted down the halls of all the important Wall Street banking firms. Rafe de la Gueronniere, a top Wall Street trader and friend of mine, was

Alan C. "Ace" Greenberg, head of Bear Stearns, is a legendary cigar smoker on Wall Street. (Photo by David Burnett/CONTACT Press Images, New York)

known for striding through the J. P. Morgan and Paine Webber bond trading floors with an ever-present Partagas Double Corona that made him look like a smoking Sherman tank on the move. Today, executives who want to smoke are confined to their own well-ventilated offices. Lou Gerstner, chairman of IBM is a smoker; so are press baron Mort Zuckerman and

Richard B. Fisher, Chairman of Morgan Stanley & Co. According to *Cigar Aficionado*, Bernd Pischetsrieder, chairman of the Board of Management of BMW AG, favors Davidoff Dom Perignons and Romeo y Julieta Belicosos. Alan "Ace" Greenberg, chairman of Bear Stearns & Co., has several passions, including hunting and doing magic tricks, but his supreme

Barnaby Conrad III, Macanudo in Paris, 1992, collage and ink on paper, 9 $^7/_{16}$ x 11 $^1/_2$ inches. (Modernism Gallery, San Francisco)

pleasure is cigars. Perhaps not surprisingly, he has done deals with billionaire Ron Perleman, who owns Revlon, Marvel Entertainment, and Consolidated Cigar Company, which produces Montecristo, Te-Amo, Por Larrañaga, H. Upmann, Primo del Rey, and other top brands. Perelman's midtown Manhattan office has a painting by Warhol and needlepoint cushions saying, "No Guts, No Glory" and "Love Me, Love My Cigar."

Perelman's holding company, MacAndrew & Forbes Holdings Inc., first bought Consolidated Cigar in 1984 for $118 million, then sold it in 1988 for $138 million; they reacquired the company in 1992 for $188 million—at a higher price to be sure, but the company's value had risen and it was perfect timing to catch the cigar renaissance.

Left: A humidor and leather carrying case by Nat Sherman of New York. (Photo by Rick Bolen) Below: Hedge fund manager Rafe de la Gueronniere and Duncan Chapman of Butler, Chapman & Co., Inc., smoking with Dale DeGroff at the Promenade Bar of the Rainbow Room in Manhattan. (Photo by Veronique Louis)

Some executives have felt enough anti-smoking pressure to speak out; Philip H. Geier, Jr., chairman and CEO of the Interpublic Group of Companies, Inc., a $2 billion advertising and communications holding company, went so far as to write an op-ed piece for *The New York Times* entitled, "Where Smokers Can Breathe Free." Geier puffs several Cubans a day and considers them an essential tool for mental concentration. Still, he no longer feels comfortable being photographed with a cigar in the company's annual report. Steven Florio, president of Condé Nast Publications, Inc., only smokes his Hoyo de Monterrey and La Gloria Cubana brands in his well-ventilated office, or when he's sailing. Jerry Reinsdorf, an Arizona-based real estate magnate who owns the Chicago Bulls and the Chicago White Sox, smokes seven cigars a day—but rarely in his Phoenix mansion, by edict of his wife.

Gangsters in old Hollywood movies always wore broad-striped suits and smoked big cigars. So did real gangsters like Al Capone. Capos, wise guys, and knock-around guys still smoke cigars, whether in restaurants or prison. Anthony "Fat Tony" Salerno, late boss of the Genovese crime family, believed to be the mastermind behind the disappearance of Jimmy Hoffa, enjoyed cigars by Primo del Rey, Davidoff, and H. Upmann. He served time, but had ways of getting

Opposite: Lefty Remini giving fighter Tami Mauriello a pep talk before a bout at Madison Square Garden in 1950. (UPI/Bettmann)

them inside the pen. Sometimes, it isn't wise for a wise guy to linger over a cigar. After lunching at Joe and Mary's restaurant in Brooklyn, Carmine "Lilo" Galante had just lit up a Presidente when he was rather indelicately shot by Anthony "Bruni" Indelicato. This, clearly, was one case where cigar smoking was hazardous to his health.

Mobster Al Capone was in a good mood in 1952. (UPI/ Bettmann Newsphotos)

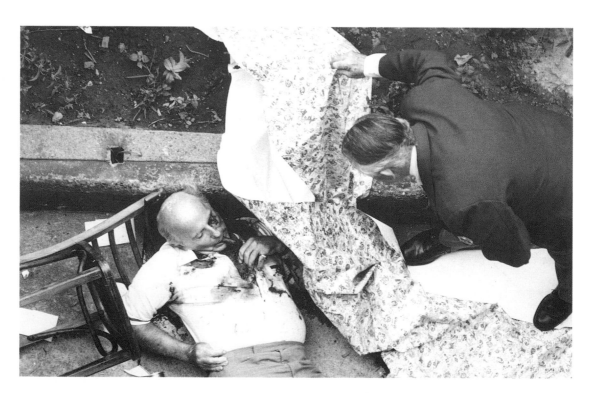

Underworld godfather Carmine Galante lingered too long over a good cigar at a Brooklyn restaurant on July 12, 1979, and was shot rather indelicately by Anthony "Bruni" Indelicato. Note the cigar still in his mouth. (UPI/Bettmann Newsphotos)

CHAPTER THREE

THE CIGAR IN LITERATURE, HOLLYWOOD, AND ART

The most futile and disastrous day seems well spent when it is reviewed through the blue, fragrant smoke of a Havana cigar.

EVELYN WAUGH

Evelyn Waugh, author of Brideshead Revisited, wrote in his diaries: "Worked quite well. Drank good wine and smoked good cigars." (Popperfoto, London)

Cigars owe much to art and literature, and vice versa. They figured importantly in social caricatures by nineteenth-century French artists such as Honoré Daumier and Sulpice Guillaume Chevalier, while Jane Austen, Honoré Balzac, Henry James, and Charles Dickens created fictional characters who sometimes revealed their truest desires while smoking cigars. William Makepeace Thackeray loved a good cigar, calling it "that great unbosomer of secrets." His novel *Vanity Fair* is full of smoking references such as this wonderful little courtship scene:

> "You don't mind my cigar, do you Miss Sharp?" Miss Sharp loved the smell of a cigar out of doors beyond everything in the world—and she just tasted one too in the prettiest way possible, gave a little puff, and a little scream and a little giggle, and restored the delicacy to the Captain, who twirled his

Ted Allan's classic photo of Groucho Marx, 1935. (©Ted Allan/The Kobal Collection, New York)

moustache, and straightway puffed it into a blaze that glowed quite red in the dark plantation, and swore—"Jove—aw—Gad—aw—it's the finest seegaw I ever smoked in the world—aw," for his intellect and conversation were alike brilliant and becoming to a heavy young dragoon.

Thackeray always began his writing day with a cigar. As reported in *Tobacco Talk* (1897), "Often he would light a cigar, and after pacing the room for a few minutes, would put the unsmoked remnant on the mantlepiece, and resume his work with increased cheerfulness, as if he had gathered fresh inspiration from the gentle odours of tobacco."

William Makepeace Thackeray smoked constantly while writing his novels such as Vanity Fair. (Corbis/Bettmann)

Right: Anthony Trollope, one of the most prolific British novelists of the last century, posed for his photograph with a cigar in his mouth. (Culver Pictures)

Dickens was not so great a cigar smoker as his friend Thackeray. Nevertheless, it was Dickens not Thackeray who eventually inspired the name of a cigar brand in 1897, *The Pickwick*. Dickens was obsessed by hospitals, jails, and asylums; once in a Lausanne clinic he met a young patient who was deaf and dumb but somehow able to communicate such a passion for cigars that Dickens gave the boy all the cigars he had in his pockets. He then left a sum of money "to be expended in cigars for the smoking patient." Later, when the director tried to rekindle a memory of the author's visit in the invalid, it was impossible. "Ah," said Dickens, "if only I had brought a cigar with me! This would have established my identity."

Rudyard Kipling, who was awarded the Nobel Prize in 1907, probably cost himself a knighthood

MR ANTHONY TROLLOPE
STEREOSCOPIC COY   COPYRIGHT

with the poem about the man who says, "A woman's just a woman, but a good cigar's a smoke."

Across the Atlantic, Samuel Clemens, better known as Mark Twain, had a cigar named for him, and the box label depicts the author flanked by his two most famous creations, Tom Sawyer and Huckleberry Finn. Clemens was a constant cigar smoker, consuming upwards of 20 per day. "I smoke in moderation," he said. "Only one cigar at a time." He deliberately sought out the cheapest, worst-smelling cigars. Though Clemens began smoking heavily at the age of eight, he lived a life nearly free of illness until his death by heart failure at age 74.

In *Following the Equator*, Twain wrote about trying to cut back: "I pledged myself to smoke but one cigar a day. I kept the cigar waiting until bedtime, then I had a luxurious time with it. But desire persecuted me every day and all day long. I found myself hunting for larger cigars. . . . within the month my cigar had grown to such proportions I could have used it as a crutch."

Samuel Clemens, better known as Mark Twain, smoked constantly while he wrote. "I ordinarily smoke fifteen cigars during my five hours' labours, and if my interest reaches the enthusiastic point, I smoke more." (UPI/Bettmann)

Mark Twain appeared on a cigar label with two of his creations, Huck Finn and Tom Sawyer.

H. L. Mencken (1880-1956) standing with cigar in hand aboard the S.S. Bremen in 1930. The most powerful journalist of his time was the son of a well-known Maryland cigar maker. (UPI/Bettmann)

Twain's wife, Olivia, prevailed on him and he did quit for several miserable months, which nearly led him to writer's block.

While struggling with a stubborn draft of *Roughing It*, he recanted. "Then I gave up the fight, resumed my three hundred cigars [a month], burned the six chapters, and wrote the book in three months, without any bother or difficulty. I ordinarily smoke fifteen cigars during my five hours' labours, and if my interest reaches the enthusiastic point, I smoke more. I smoke with all my might, and allow no intervals." (Fittingly, about ten years ago, a stamp collector bought two old cigar boxes filled with postcards and envelopes—and they turned out to be valuable letters from Twain to his daughter.)

The journalist H. L. Mencken, son of prominent Baltimore cigar maker August Mencken, smoked cigars all his life with great pleasure. As a young man he spent three and a half unhappy years working in the family business before his father's death liberated him to pursue a career so brilliant that Alistair Cooke would later call him, "the most volcanic newspaperman this country has ever known." People used to crowd around him at political conventions just to watch him type out his scathing and wise commentary.

During his first years as a columnist, Mencken faced down a group of women who complained that cigar smoking should be prohibited on Baltimore streetcars,

FROM SKETCHES AND TRAVELS IN LONDON

by William Makepeace Thackeray (1896)

Honest men, with pipes or cigars in their mouths, have great physical advantages in conversation. You may stop talking if you like—but the breaks of silence never seem disagreeable, being filled up by the puffing of the smoke—hence there is no awkwardness in resuming the conversation—no straining for effect—sentiments are delivered in a grave easy manner—the cigar harmonizes the society, and soothes at once the speaker and the subject whereon he converses. I have no doubt that it is from the habit of smoking that Turks and American Indians are such monstrous well-bred men. The pipe draws wisdom from the lips of the philosopher, and shuts up the mouth of the foolish: it generates a style of conversation, contemplative, thoughtful, benevolent, and unaffected: in fact, dear Bob, I must out with it—I am an old smoker. At home I have done it up the chimney rather than not do it (the which I own is a crime). I vow and believe that the cigar has been one of the greatest creature-comforts of my life—a kind companion, a gentle stimulant, an amiable anodyne, a cementer of friendship. May I die if I abuse that kindly weed which has given me so much pleasure!

(Corbis/Bettmann)

HABANA

writing: "Women in general are not nearly so delicate as romance makes them. A woman who can stand half an hour of the Lexington fish market is well able to face a few blasts of tobacco smoke." Mencken's fine biographer, Marion Elizabeth Rogers, notes that although Mencken added, "not one in 10,000 [women] can tell the difference between good tobacco and bad," it was all a case of principle and liberty rather than misogyny—for in another instance he was quick to defend a suffragette who had been arrested for lighting up a cigarette on a train.

Psychoanalysis may owe a lot to cigars. In the fall of 1902, Sigmund Freud and his colleagues met every Wednesday in Freud's Vienna home at 19 Bergasse. In meetings of the "Vienna Psycho-Analytical Society," Freud would seat his colleagues around a long table—with plenty of ashtrays—where theories were launched, challenged, and developed amid a swirl of cigar smoke. Freud's son Martin recalled the room being "so thick with smoke it seemed a wonder that human beings had been able to live in it for hours, let alone speak in it without choking."

Before his marriage to Martha Bernays, Freud wrote to her that "Smoking is indis-

pensable if one has nothing to kiss." Freud was seldom without a cigar and typically smoked 15 per day. As patients lay on the couch, he sat behind them in an armchair, smoking and taking notes. The psychoanalyst Raymond De Saussure underwent analysis by Freud in the 1920s and recalled the experience in a memoir, *Freud As We Knew Him*: "One was won over by the atmosphere of his office, a rather dark room, which opened onto a courtyard. Light came not from

the windows but from the brilliance of that lucid, discerning mind. Contact was established only by means of his voice and the odor of the cigars he ceaselessly smoked."

For Freud it was unthinkable not to smoke. When his 17-year-old nephew Harry declined a cigar, Freud solemnly advised: "My

Opposite page: Sigmund Freud (1856-1939), photographed in 1922. The founder of psychoanalysis, Freud smoked 20 cigars a day and encouraged all his colleagues to smoke them. Before his marriage to Martha Bernays, he wrote her that "Smoking is indispensable if one has nothing to kiss." (Library of Congress)

boy, smoking is one of the greatest and cheapest enjoyments in life, and to decide in advance not to smoke, I can only feel sorry for you."

Freud began smoking at the age of 24, picking up the pleasure enjoyed by his father, a hard-working fabric manufacturer who lived to be 81. He always associated the cigar

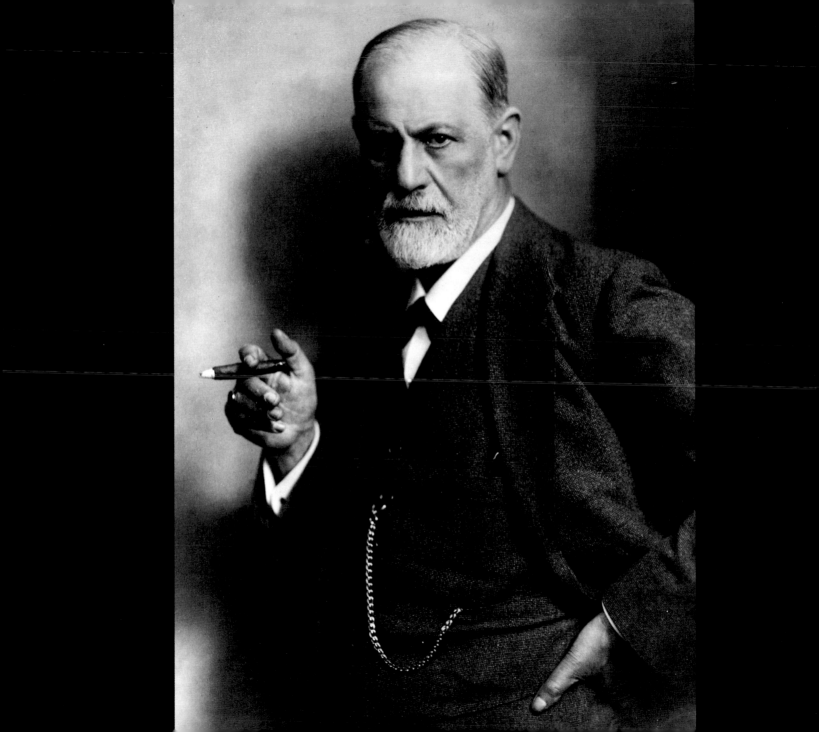

with tenacity and self-control. Late in his life Freud said that cigars "served me for precisely fifty years as protection and a weapon in the combat of life. . . . I owe to the cigar a great intensification of my capacity to work and a facilitation of my self-control." Writing in a *Cigar Aficionado* article, Evan J. Elkin asserts, "Clearly Freud saw a connection between cigars, patrician authority, and success."

Freud lived a highly ritualized life in which cigars were always present. He rose at 7 A.M., saw patients from 8 A.M. to noon, lunched with his family, then walked around Vienna for an hour, usually stopping to visit his favorite tobacconist. He kept a diary throughout his life and carefully recorded all his cigar purchases. After playing cards with his sister-in-law or taking a coffee and newspaper at a local cafe, he returned home for dinner with his family. Afterward, Freud would retire to his study, light a cigar, and resume

Opposite: A fanciful cigar box by San Francisco artist Scooter for the mature Mickey Mouse fan. (Photo by Rick Bolen)

the writing of his seminal works. He usually smoked a *trabuco*, which was a small, mild cigar favored by the Austrians, but he preferred Don Pedros and Reina Cubanas, which he purchased on visits across the Bavarian border to Berchtesgaden.

Freud smoked until the end of his life, which came at 83. He had moved to London in 1938 after the Nazis occupied Vienna. There is a photograph of him sitting at his desk at 20 Maresfield Gardens as he worked on the manuscript of his last book, *Moses and Monotheism*, with a cigar in hand. Before dying, he bequeathed his brother Alexander his stock of fine cigars, and wrote: "Your seventy-second birthday finds us on the verge of separating after long years of living together. I hope it is not going to be a separation forever, but the future—always uncertain—is at the moment especially difficult to foresee. I would like you to take over the good cigars which have been accumulating with me over the years, as you can still indulge in such pleasure, I no longer."

The cigar has been a dramatic prop in showbiz for over a century. Long before movies, the nineteenth-century American showman P. T. Barnum presented the midget General Tom Thumb in his circus act as "The Smallest Man in the World." The little man was smoking an enormous Havana cigar. The cigar appeared in several Charlie Chaplin films. In *City Lights* Chaplin jumps out of a limousine (borrowed from a million-

aire drunk) to steal a recently cast-off stogie from a bum. In *The Gold Rush*, the little tramp has struck it rich in the Yukon and is returning first class by steamer, when a fellow passenger drops a spent cigar; though now a millionaire, Charlie can't shake old habits, and jumps on the smoking castoff with undiminished relish. Laurel and Hardy, Harold Lloyd, and many other silent stars developed sight gags—cigars slammed in doors, holes burned in clothing—for cigars. Will Fowler once told me how his Uncle Claude, better known as W. C. Fields, worked the cigar into his role as riverboat captain in the 1935 film *Mississippi*. "He would steer the huge wheel slowly, staring directly ahead. Each time a wheel handle threatened to knock the cigar, he would allow the cigar to snap up, then settle down, then snap up again."

A silver carrying case from Nat Sherman of New York. (Photo by Rick Bolen)

Opposite. Comedians Milton Berle, Joey Bishop, and Jimmy Durante blew smoke while rehearsing for President Kennedy's inaugural ball in 1961. (UPI/Bettmann).

Bertolt Brecht extolled the cheap cigar, probably fitting for the author of *The Threepenny Opera*. The German playwright dreamed of creating an "epic smoke-theater" in which the audience would be more stimulated to artistic reverie if allowed to smoke during performances. Ernst Lubitsch, a German

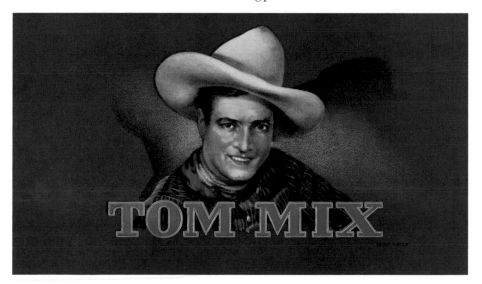

Cowboy film star Tom Mix had a label named for him.

FROM THE IDIOT BY FYODOR DOSTOYEVSKY (1868)

(Translated by Henry and Olga Carlisle)

(Culver Pictures)

It's a stupid story and can be told in a couple of words," began the general complacently. "Two years ago—yes, almost two—shortly after the opening of the—whatever it was railway, I—being already in civilian clothes at the time—I was taking care of some extremely important business about my separation from the service. I bought a first-class ticket, got on, sat down, started smoking. That is, I went on smoking the cigar I had lit already. I was alone in the compartment. Smoking isn't forbidden, but then it isn't exactly allowed either; that is, it's sort of half-allowed, as things like that usually are, and of course it depends on the individual. The window was open. All of a sudden, just before the whistle, two ladies sit down right across from me with a lapdog. They'd been late getting on. One of them was most elegantly dressed in light blue, the other more modestly in black silk and a cape. Not bad to look at, either one. Very haughty. Spoke in English. Of course I go right on smoking. That is, I did give it a thought but went right on smoking anyway, letting the smoke go out the window, since it was open. The lapdog is sitting there in the pale-blue-lady's lap. A little thing no bigger than my fist, black with little white paws—quite an oddity. Had a silver collar with a motto. I pay no attention, except I do notice that the ladies are apparently displeased. By the cigar of course. One of them glares at me through a lorgnette. Tortoise shell. I go right on paying no attention—naturally, because they don't say anything! If they'd said something, warned me, asked me—because, after all, people are capable of speech! But not a noise from them. Then, suddenly—and, mind you, without the slightest warning, with absolutely no warning at all, just as if she had lost her mind—the pale-blue-one snatches the cigar out of my hand and flings it out of the window. The train is racing along, and I'm staring at her like a half-wit. The woman is savage, she's a wild woman; I mean she is absolutely primitive. What's more, she's a big round plump woman, a blond with pink cheeks (too pink in fact), and her eyes are flashing at me. So without a word, I lean forward, and with exceptional courtesy, with perfect politeness, you might even say with elegance, I get hold of the lapdog with two fingers by the scruff of the neck and heave it out of the window after the cigar. It let out just one yelp. The train was racing along—"

"You monster!" cried Nastassya Filippovna, laughing and clapping her hands like a little girl.

"Bravo! Bravo!" shouted Ferdyshchenko. Ptitsyn, too, was smiling, although he had been highly displeased by the arrival of the general. Even Kolya laughed and joined in, crying "Bravo!"

"And I was right, too. I was absolutely right!" the triumphant general continued, with great warmth. "Because if cigars are prohibited in railway cars, dogs are all the more!"

low comedian who became Hollywood's most brilliant purveyor of sophisticated sex comedy, chain-smoked cigars while making *Trouble In Paradise*, *Ninotchka*, and *The Shop Around the Corner*. According to Cuban novelist G. Cabrera Infante, Lubitsch died in bed with a blond astride him and a cigar still smoking in his ashtray. Producer Jack Warner was smoking a Panatela made by Hoyo de Monterrey on the day he won his famous *banco* of a hundred million francs at the Palm Beach Casino in Cannes. Today, the slightly gnawed cigar is conserved in a silver box at the Casino as a memento of the occasion. Darryl Zanuck was such a connoisseur of the cigar that before Castro's arrival he owned his own *vega* (plantation) in the Vuelta Abajo, the heart of Cuba's tobacco region.

Orson Welles and Alfred Hitchcock smoked continually on the set. Welles once said he made movies to be able to smoke for free: "That's why I write [in] so many cigar-smoking heroes and villains who chomp their cigars." The tradition has been carried on today by directors Francis Ford Coppola and John Milius. Spaghetti western maestro Sergio Leone encouraged Clint Eastwood to smoke a slender Italian *cheroot*—and made spitting into the desert dust a trademark gesture. Cellu-

loid thespians Roger Moore, Bill Cosby, Chevy Chase, Pierce Brosnan, Robert Duvall, Michael Nouri, James Coburn and Robert De Niro are known to favor Cubans.

"If I'd taken my doctor's advice and quit smoking when he advised me to, I wouldn't have lived to go to his funeral," said the late George Burns at age 98. Burns was the only celebrity permitted to press his cigar into the cement at Mann's Chinese Theater on Hollywood Boulevard. Even at a hundred years old, Burns still smoked about 10 cigars a day. "I smoke a domestic cigar. It's a good cigar. It's called the El Producto," he told Arthur Marx (son of Groucho). Presumably the durable hoofer could afford better than a machine-made product, but in Burns' case the show's the thing: "Now the reason I smoke a domestic cigar is because the more expensive Havana cigars are tightly packed. They go out on stage while I'm doing my act. The El Producto stays lit . . . If you have to stop your act to keep lighting your cigar, the audience goes out. That's why I smoke El Productos. They stay lit."

Born Nathan Birnbaum, Burns was the ninth of twelve children in a poor family on the Lower East Side of New York City. When his father, a substitute cantor at a synagogue, died, Burns went to work at age seven selling newspapers and making candy syrups. After forming a singing quartet with neighborhood kids, he quit school in the fourth grade, went into showbiz, and changed his name to George Burns. At first, he confessed in *Cigar Aficionado,* "When they saw me walking down the street smoking a cigar, they'd say, 'Hey, that 14-year-old kid must be going places.' Of course, it's also a good prop on the stage. . . . When you can't think of what you are supposed to say next, you take a puff on your cigar until you do think of your next line."

W. C. Fields smoking on the set of It's a Gift, *1935. (Culver Pictures)*

Opposite: Mark Stock, The Artist of the Twentieth Century, *1996, oil and acrylic on panel, 16 $^1/_2$ x 14 $^3/_4$ inches. (Modernism Gallery, San Francisco)*

Milton Berle smoked his first cigar at age 13 in Havana in 1921. Born in 1908 to a befuddled failure of a father and an ambitious mother, Milton became a child actor. He was on a cruise to Cuba with his mother and sister when a street vendor sold him a cigar for 12 cents. "I didn't know you were not supposed to inhale a cigar. Pretty soon I got sick to my stomach and started to

Orchestra leader Count Basie rehearsing for his 1981 Carnegie Hall appearance. (UPI/ Bettmann)

throw up," he told Arthur Marx in a recent interview. But he was hooked, and from then on smoked only the best cigars. At 88 years old, he still smokes five Cohibas a day.

Jack Nicholson began smoking cigarettes as a teenager, quit when he married Sandra Knight in 1962, and stayed nicotine-free for ten years. While filming *The Last Detail* in 1972 he wanted the naval petty officer character he played to smoke cigars; the film went well, but he was soon smoking cigarettes again. He gave them up for cigars in 1991, figuring that "the only way to break a bad habit was to replace it with a better habit." He shares his appreciation for fine cigars with friends Danny DeVito, Michael Douglas, Robert De Niro, and Peter Fonda, but also alone at home listening to classical music. He never smokes around his children and is considerate in restaurants. Nicholson favors Cubans—Romeo y Julietas, Cohiba robustos and Montecristos—even on the golf course. (He claims cigars help his concentration and nerves, lowering his handicap to 12.)

Opposite: Songwriters Lorenz Hart and Richard Rodgers. (Culver Pictures)
Below: George Burns as seen by New York Times *caricaturist Al Hirshfeld in 1977. (Courtesy Margo Feiden Gallery, New York)*

For Francis Ford Coppola, cigar smoking is nearly a spiritual connection with his late father, the composer Carmine Coppola. "I started smoking these little Italian cigars just so there was some of that smell in the air," he said wistfully. Coppola's father once went to Cuba and was paid entirely in Cohibas. Francis has been there to teach at the National Film School and met Castro. Among the director's most treasured objects is a gold and silver cigar cutter that had once belonged to Jack Warner of Warner Bros.; it had been given to Warner by Lord Mountbatten, former viceroy of India, who was assassinated in 1979.

The most notable cigar film of recent years is *Smoke* (1995), written by Paul Auster and directed by Wayne Wang. The central figure in the story is the proprietor of the Brooklyn

Cigar Shop, Auggie Wren (played by Harvey Keitel), who on first appearance is a rather ordinary man. Auggie's obsession is photographing the view from the street corner every morning at precisely eight o'clock. William Hurt plays Paul, a recently widowed writer who drops in regularly to chat and buy cigars. Paul's favorite brand is Schimmelpenninck, which happens to be the favorite smoke of novelist and screenwriter Paul Auster. The movie's main plot is a get-rich-quick scheme doomed to failure—a shipment of illegal Cuban cigars in which Auggie has invested his life savings. In the course of a complex tale of love lost and found, and the search for life's purpose, the male characters display their better, kinder natures while savoring cigars.

Great artists have smoked cigars: Pierre-Auguste Renoir, Kees Van Dongen, Pablo Picasso, Marcel Duchamp, and David Hockney come immediately to mind. Frank Stella has recently commenced a series of sculptures that take their inspiration simply from the swirl of smoke rising from a cigar.

But the great popular cigar art is the labels and the boxes that present them. In 1830, the banking firm of H. Upmann began shipping cigars to its directors in London in sealed cedar boxes emblazoned with the bank's emblem. When the bank went into the cigar business full force, Upmann rapidly set a trend for packaging in the industry. In 1837 Ramon Allones, a Spanish immigrant to Cuba, began printing colorful lithographic labels as a way of differentiating brands. It spawned an industry that took stone lithography to new heights of quality. There were many literary references, too. In 1935, the Menendez family, owners of H. Upmann, created the Montecristo brand as a tribute to the fictional hero of Alexander Dumas's novel *The Count of Montecristo*. Today *vistas*, as the colorful images on boxtops are called, are avidly collected in America and Europe, and vintage examples fetch thousands of dollars apiece for rarities.

Surprisingly the man who invented the cigar band, Gustave Bock, was neither Cuban nor Spanish, but Dutch. In 1850, Bock developed the ingenious—if obvious—idea of labeling his cigars to distinguish them from other brands. Soon monarchs, presidents, state officials, and leading world figures were honored to have their faces on cigar bands.

At the turn of the century, cigars showed up in that truly American art form: the comic strips. "The Katzenjammer Kids" introduced the cigar-chomping Der Captain in 1897; the racetrack fanatic Mutt of "Mutt and Jeff" first

Opposite: Edward G. Robinson smoked just about everywhere. (Springer/Bettmann Film Archive) Below: Paul Newman took a break from filming Hombre *(1967) to have a smoke with a cigar store Indian. (UPI/Bettmann)*

lit up a cigar in 1907; and the hen-pecked Jiggs of "Bringing Up Father" lit up in 1913. Since then Barney Google, Moon Mullins, and Dagwood's boss Mr. Dithers have been well-known heavy smokers. Little Orphan Annie's guardian Daddy

Warbucks usually sported a cigar as did Dick Tracy's partner Sam Catchem.

In the early days, the cigar was associated with carefree pleasure in comics; by midcentury it symbolized an ornery sense of capitalist power or harsh authority. Brenda Starr's editor smoked them, as did Spiderman's cantankerous boss; *Daily Planet* editor Perry White chomped them when Lois Lane failed to get a good story on Superman.

Walt Kelly, creator of "Pogo," smoked Cubans and kept his art supplies in emptied boxes of La Corona Queen produced by Alvarez Lopez and Company. Rube Goldberg, whose cartoons lampooned technology run amok, was an avid smoker. In his strip "Shoe," cartoonist Jeff MacNelly features a strange-looking duck named P. Martin Shoemaker who puffs ferociously on his cigar while typing his newspaper column, "The Cigar Corner Sewer," which appears in the *Treetops Tattler*. In one example of his shared bits of wisdom, Shoe writes: "To fully appreciate fine cigars,

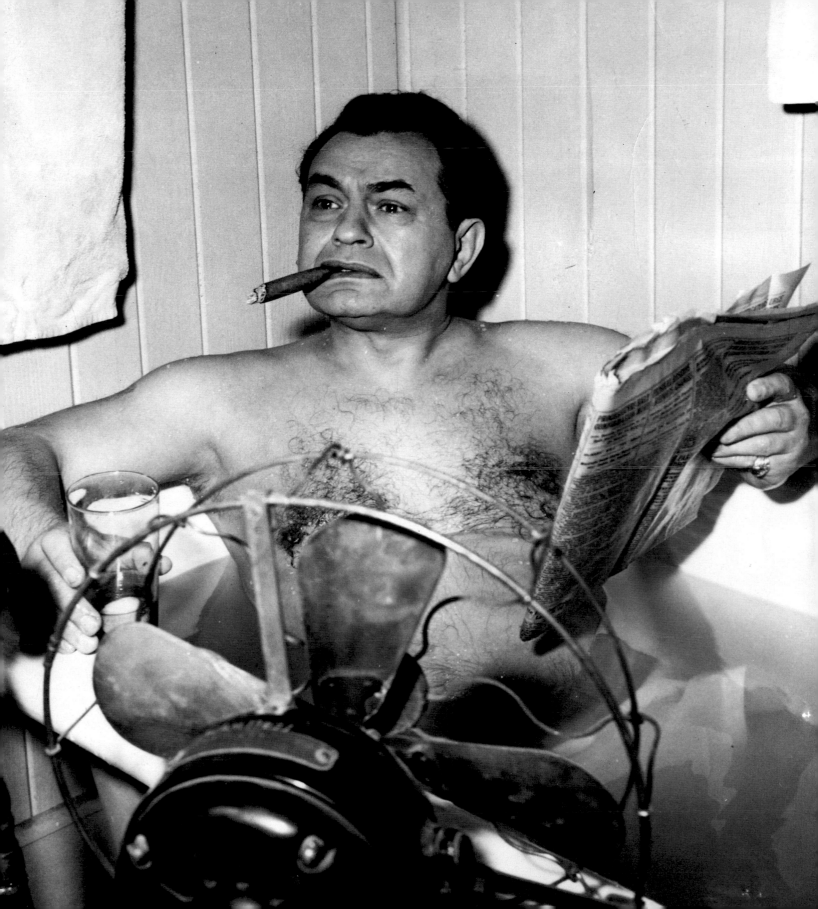

it's important to recognize the various types of cigars. There are two basic categories of cigar. The lit and the unlit." Shoe is an alter ego of his 48-year-old creator, MacNelly, who smokes cigars while he sketches his panels. "The cigar suggests to me a kind of worldly gruffness," says MacNelly, "so that's why I installed one in Shoe's mouth." In the strip a reader writes a letter to Shoe asking for advice: "Dear Mr. Shoemaker: I'd like to enjoy cigar smoking on a regular basis but I find that they burn my tongue. What can I do?" Shoe replies: "Next time try putting the other end in your mouth."

Arnold Schwarzenegger wields a rather large cigar cutter. (Photo by M.Neveux, Shooting Star) Opposite: William Holden starred in Billy Wilder's film Stalag 17. (Paramount Pictures)

Cartoonist Jeff MacNelly drawing his strip, "Shoe." (Photo by Dennis Brack/Black Star)

CHAPTER FOUR

THE CUBAN MYSTIQUE

The Vuelta Abajo is a natural hothouse, just as the whole island of Cuba is a natural humidor.

BERNARD WOLFE, FORMER SECRETARY TO LEON TROTSKY

It was eight o'clock at night when the Cuban Air jet, a Russian-made Yak-140, touched down at Havana's José Martí International Airport. One of the few Americans flying in from Nassau, I was unsure of what awaited me. My arrival, however, was the fulfillment of a long-held dream—the equivalent of the Muslim going to Mecca, the artist visiting the Louvre, the wine enthusiast seeing Bordeaux for the first time.

The Cuban customs formalities were surprisingly brief; after all, few foreigners wish to emigrate to this country. Americans have been visiting Cuba legally and illegally (departing from Nassau, Canada, and Mexico) for years. Thirty minutes later, a taxi deposited me at the Hotel Plaza, just off the Plaza Mayor. After a quick shower and change of clothes, I roamed the streets of old Havana, alternately thrilled and saddened by the shabby grandeur. It was as if several *arrondissements* of nineteenth-century Paris had been transported here and left to decay for 35 years. The faded, crumbling beauty was captivating, eerie, and ultimately intoxicating. The island's economy is in shambles, and Cuba's 11 million people are poor. With the failure of communism, the Soviets stopped making their $5 billion per year subsidies, and Cuba's economy shrank 50 percent overnight. After sugar,

After sugar cane, cigars are one of Cuba's prime cash exports. (Photo by Stephen Ferry/ The Gamma Liaison Network, New York)

nickel, fish, and tourism, cigars remain the premier cash export for the country.

Two blocks from my hotel I found the Floridita, Ernest Hemingway's favorite wa-
tering hole. A well-dressed door-
man let me into a clean, well-
lighted place for nostalgia. A

friendly, all-but-toothless bartender in a crisp white jacket made an excellent daiquiri
and revived my rusty Spanish. On the wall were photographs of Hemingway with Erroll
Flynn, Gary Cooper, and in an awkward embrace with *El Lider Maximo*, Fidel Castro,
taken just before Papa left Cuba forever.

*A fine selection of Cuban
cigars including the Partagas
Lusitania, H. Upmann
Monarch, Romeo & Julieta
Prince of Wales, Romeo &
Julieta Churchill, Davidoff
Dom Perignon, Cohiba
Esplendido, Bolivar
Corona Gigante, and the
Partagas Lusitania.
(Photo by Rick Bolen)*

The Floridita is still a beautiful bar, and it was good to hear Spanish spoken, but it was sad because no Cubans (save for employees) were allowed in this place unless accompanied by a tourist; no Cubans, except Castro's inner circle, could even afford to come in here. I ate fish for dinner in the dining room, then went back to the bar for a snifter of seven-year-old rum. I spied boxes of cigars—*puros* as they are always called in Cuba—behind the bar. A moment later I was puffing a Cohiba Lancero. I was nearly giddy with the pleasure of being able to smoke freely. After another rum, I bought a couple more Cohibas. Walking back to the hotel, I took pleasure in simply feeling their bulk in my pocket.

For the next few days I explored old Havana, reveling in the city's rich past—a saga of pirates, slave traders, and merchants lubricated on rum and perfumed by cigar smoke. The few Cubans I met were warm, polite people living under an oppressive regime that they hope will change; but every time I saw a soldier on the corner or a wall painted with political slogans (*"Venceremos"* and *"Revolucion o muerte"*) I was reminded that Cuba is still a totalitarian state where there is no free speech, few property rights, and virtually no tolerance for free enterprise.

When Castro came to power in 1959 he nationalized the sugar and cigar industries. In the frenzied honeymoon of revolutionary fervor, Castro initially declared that the individual brands of the great cigar companies were nothing more than capitalist selfishness. In place, he proposed a single cigar made "for the people" with only slight variations, until

FROM HOLY SMOKE

by G. Cabrera Infante (1985)

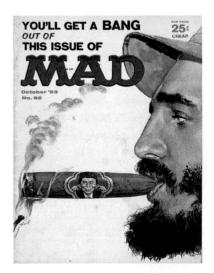

I was once with Castro on an impromptu visit to a cattle ranch on an island off the eastern coast of Cuba. When night fell I watched a Western on television. Castro came into the room to watch the show and immediately he asked: 'Who has a cigar?' I had four Havanas in my shirt pocket, very visible in the moonlight of the prairie. So I said I had. I *had* to. I also had to give him a cigar. As he got involved in the yarn of singing cowboys and wagons and their masters, Castro asked for a second cigar. Then for a third. Fortunately I knew that *Wagonmaster* was Ford's shortest Western, barely ninety minutes long. It was soon over. Castro stood up, all uniformed and pistoled six feet of him, and commented: 'Too many songs and not enough Indians.' We all agreed. Our Prime Minister was our first film critic too. He was also the sole talker, as usual: he made us turn the room into a Cuban chorus. Fortunately he was tired that night and soon went to bed, followed by his bodyguards. But before leaving he turned to me and said: 'I see we have one Indian left.' He was pointing at my pocket and not at my head: he meant my last cigar. He referred to it as if it were one more Apache. 'Do you mind if I borrow it?' What could I say? Don't mind if you do, *Comandante*? I surrendered my last cigar. When he left with that borrowed Por Larrañaga that he never paid me back, I turned to the TV set. It was off but around it on the floor were the other three *tabacos*, dead soldiers all but barely smoked. Obviously prime ministers make lousy smokers.

fellow revolutionary Ché Guevara counseled against this. Meanwhile, the owners of companies such as H. Upmann, Romeo y Julieta, Partagas, Punch, and Hoyo de Monterrey fled to Florida, the Dominican Republic, Jamaica, and Honduras where they continue to make great cigars. The Cuban mystique is still strong, but many experts now debate convincingly that cigars made in Honduras and the Dominican Republic are equal or superior.

Within months after the takeover, emissaries from Havana visited the late Zino Davidoff in Geneva to ask what could be done to bolster sales. Davidoff told them that the strength of Cuba's cigar industry lay in its diversity of cigars—similar to the advice that revolutionary Ché Guevara had given Castro. Chastened, the government reversed its policy and brought back the famed brand names again—even though the real owners were already using those names in exile.

The Cubans are still able to produce some of the greatest cigars in the world. The heart of its industry is a small area called the Vuelta Abajo, about 100 miles west of Havana. It contains many small *vegas* or plantations of tobacco totaling just 100,000 acres.

The finest tobacco in the world is grown in the Pinar del Rio region of western Cuba. (Photo by David Burnett/CONTACT Press Images, New York)

One morning I joined a bus tour headed out to Pinar del Rio in the tobacco heart-land. We headed west as rain threatened, traveling through countryside planted with sugarcane. The rich bottomlands were rimmed with abrupt hills that resembled parts of Malaysia and Thailand. The reddish sandy loam is perfect for tobacco. Although it rains 65 inches a year, during the November to February tobacco season, a scant 8 inches fall. It is a labor intensive industry, with each plant being tended by hand nearly 170 times in the 120-day cycle. Once harvested, tobacco leaves are strung on poles in a barn and allowed to dry for 45 to 60 days, during which time the bright green leaves turn brown. They are then bunched, flattened, and laid down to ferment naturally, a process generat-ing temperatures of 112 degrees. No chemicals are used in the process. The leaves are then sorted for size and fermented some more. Because of this process, cigar leaf is much lower in acidity, tar, and nicotine than cigarette tobacco. The leaves are then

Selling cigars on the black market in Cuba. (Photo by Stephen Ferry/The Gamma Liaison Network, New York)

shipped to factories; those of the highest quality are reserved for cigars destined for export, those of lower quality set aside for domestic consumption.

Back in Havana I found the Partagas factory standing opposite the former Cuban Senate, a building modeled after the Capitol building in Washington, D.C. Today it is a library—Fidel does all the political thinking for the people. The Partagas factory is a pretty building painted cream and brown, with the date 1845 visible at the top of its four stories. The company recently celebrated its 150th anniversary with a banquet attended by an international group of cigar cognoscenti.

Opposite: Wayne Thiebaud, Cigar and Shadow, *1973, oil on paper, 20 x 16 inches. (Campbell-Thiebaud Gallery, San Francisco)*

Despite a letter of introduction from my publisher, I was refused a tour of the factory and was told they were "understaffed" that day. I went to the Corona factory near the Museum of the Revolution and received the same answer. I returned to the Partagas factory the following morning with Pedro, a French-speaking friend, who finally convinced an assistant manager to show us through—but only after Pedro told him I was French-Canadian. "Okay, but no photographs," said the big gruff Partagas man.

Nevertheless, we saw every step of the complex process of the handmade cigar's birth. I was impressed by the speed with which the men and women cut wrappers with their oval

The Partagas factory in Havana has been in business since 1845. The anti-yankee sign appeared more recently. (Photo by the author)

steel blades called *chavetas*, formed their filler and binders in the wooden cigar forms called *vitoles*, and then wrapped the cigars and finished them. It is a nine-month apprenticeship before a cigar roller is a full professional, and many fail. The best end up making Romeo y Julietas and Cohibas. Originally dominated by men, the fraternity of rollers is now mostly a sorority. (The tasters, however, tend to be male.) A good cigar roller can make 100 to 130 cigars a day, spending an average of four to five minutes per cigar.

The voice of the reader droned over a faulty sound system. Reading to cigar makers is a century-old tradition, originally intended to entertain and educate the working class on the job. In the old days the readers—a position of great distinction in the factories—favored long dramatic novels of the highest standard: Victor Hugo's *Hunch-back of Notre Dame* or Dumas' *The Count of Montecristo* (which inspired the name of a famed Cuban cigar). Today it's the wisdom of Fidel Castro, the printed propaganda passing for a newspaper, or the radio. Occasionally a reader will read a cheap romantic novel, highly favored by the new sorority of rollers.

On another floor of the Partagas factory, women selected the finished cigars for color, grading them according to as many as 65 color variations, so that each cigar box will eventually contain cigars of similar hue. Then comes banding and boxing. The aroma was rich, organic, freshly intoxicating. In spite of our sullen guide, the foremen and workers on each floor greeted me warmly. Workers can smoke as many free cigars as they wish; one woman in her late seventies, as dark and sweet as a maduro cigar, showed me the 12-inch cigar she rolled and smoked every day. The 200 rollers at the Partagas factory turn out five million handmade cigars per year, so I was mildly disappointed that when we left, our Partagas guide did not offer even one sample cigar, but then Cuba for 35 years has had no need to butter up the press. Indeed it has had no press to speak of, and very little butter.

> With its unique soil and climate conditions, Cuba still produces what many connoisseurs feel are the finest cigars in the world. Among the famed brand names shown here are Cohiba, Romeo & Julieta, Partagas, Bolivar, Montecristo, Hoyo de Monterrey, Flor de Farach, and la Gloria Cubana. The cutter is by Davidoff. (Photo by Rick Bolen)

An experienced roller can produce over 120 cigars a day. (Photo by the author)

In 1979-80, the Cuban tobacco crop was stricken with the devastating Blue Mold disease, which led to a worldwide shortage of Cuban cigars the following year. As word leaked out, duty free shops around the world were besieged with capitalist desperadoes buying up the remaining stock. Tobacconists from London to Hong Kong were overwhelmed with panicked buyers. It took a year for the panic to subside.

Fidel Castro began smoking at 15 when his father introduced him to cigars made by Romeo y Julieta, H. Upmann, Bauza, and Partagas. For decades Castro was seldom photographed without a cigar in his mouth, usually the smaller Corona Especial. Then, in the 1980s, photos appeared of him smoking the Cohiba, a brand he helped develop after the Revolution.

The Cohiba started in the early 1960s when a friend brought Castro an aromatic cigar made by Eduardo Rivera Irizarri, then a director and top cigar roller at the El Laguito factory. The unknown cigar was long and slender, shaped like today's Cohiba Lancero. Intrigued, the dictator asked to meet the cigar maker. Rivera told him how he mixed the various blends in the filler and where he got the wrapper. Part of Castro's decision to designate Rivera as his personal cigar maker was that the craftsman could be trusted at a time when there were rumors of assassination attempts.

At first the cigars were produced solely for *El Commandante*'s consumption and were given away unbranded as diplomatic gifts. The Cohiba brand name first appeared in 1966, but it was not until the 1980s that Cohiba was sold commercially. Meanwhile, for the last three years Castro has been giving out a new cigar brand, Trinidad, as a diplomatic goody.

The Cohibas are still made in El Laguito's factory in the suburbs of Havana. The building looks less like an enterprise than a palace. And for good reason: this elegant neoclassical chateau was once home to the Marquez del Pinar del Rio, scion of a great

Because of the embargo, Havana is filled with ghostly American cars from the Eisenhower era. (Photo by the author)

Spanish family who became rich producing tobacco in the Vuelta Abajo region. Nationalized after the Revolution, the great house became a cigar-rolling school for women. Production grew so fast that in 1969 Rivera contacted Swiss merchant Zino Davidoff to discuss making other commercial brands. Within a year Davidoff developed a partnership with the Swiss import-export company Oettinger. Throughout the 1970s and 1980s, Davidoff stores opened in major cities around the world, including London, New York, Tokyo, Hong Kong, and Singapore. Davidoffs were made in Cuba until 1990, when Zino abruptly pulled out and moved his operations to the Dominican Republic.

To the surprise of cigar smokers and intelligence agencies, on August 26, 1985, Castro quit smoking cigars. The decision, Castro said in an interview with Marvin Shanken, was made less for his own health concerns than to demonstrate personal support for the international public health movement against smoking. Meanwhile, his one-time personal cigar maker, Eduardo Rivera, returned to cigar making in 1995 at the

Comodoro Hotel in Havana. "They were short-handed," was all he would give by explanation, but he seemed happy to be rolling again.

The U.S. embargo on Cuban-American trade remains in place. The streets of Havana are still cruised by late 1950s Chevy Bel-Airs and Buicks, Eisenhower-era relics kept running with Cuban ingenuity and handmade parts. There are also Italian sedans and flashy Japanese jeeps, but these are only available as rental vehicles for tourists. The U.S. embargo is not the cause of Cuba's economic malaise. Every other country in the world is free to trade with Cuba, from Japan and China to Mexico and Brazil to England, Germany, and France   but trading partners are skittish. Cuba's problem is that it has a system that prohibits free enterprise, stifles productivity, and is deaf to human nature.

When *Cigar Aficionado* publisher Marvin Shanken interviewed Castro in Havana in 1994, the Cuban leader asked, " You say that Clinton smokes cigars?" The American publisher answered, "Yes. He has smoked for many years. But his wife, Hillary, has created a no-smoking policy in the White House. So now he just chews cigars, it seems." Castro mulled this over. "Then I guess President Clinton and I will not be able to smoke our peace pipe or cigars in the White House."

CHAPTER FIVE

CIGARS AROUND THE WORLD

Every cigar goes up in smoke.

BRAZILIAN PROVERB

M.O. Dulach, Krov' i pesni, 1926, stone lithographic poster, 42 ¹/₂ x 28 inches. This remarkable Russian poster was made to promote the film Blood and Sand, starring Rudolph Valentino. (Modernism Gallery, San Francisco)

Cuban cigar makers abandoned their island in two great waves in the last century. For centuries their Spanish overlords had exploited the colonial laborers, treating Cuba as a feudal backwater. The 1880s brought a wave of Cuban immigration to Key West, Florida, among them cigar makers who, for a time, made that island town a powerful center of cigar manufacturing. In 1885, a number of these rollers journeyed north to found Ybor City near Tampa, and it soon sprouted hundreds of cigar manufacturers. By 1890 "Made in Tampa" on a cigar label was recognized as a sign of quality. The cigar factories in Key West languished as America turned to machine-made cigars, but old Cuban hands—or their disciples—still continue to roll the real thing in Ybor City.

World War II disrupted the Cuban tobacco trade as German U-boats prowled the Caribbean. English tobacco dealers were desperate for access to high quality cigars. The enterprising British turned to one of their colonies, Jamaica, and brands such as Temple Hall, El Caribe, and Flor del Duque were aggressively promoted. A number of Cuban

Tom McKinley, Cigar Tower, 1996, oil on board, 13 x 10 inches. (John Berggruen Gallery, San Francisco)

cigar experts set up shop on Jamaica, founding the Macanudo brand, which produces very fine cigars today.

The 1959 Cuban revolution forced most of the cigar makers to flee, their bags full of premium Cuban seed, and start over in other countries. Fortunately, tobacco-growing and cigar-making industries were already deep rooted in Honduras and the Dominican Republic. In the long run, the forced exodus of Cuban expertise may prove beneficial to cigar smokers worldwide, but it has created a controversial situation, a kind of trademark bigamy. The Cifuentes family, for example, which once owned Partagas in Havana, joined another cigar refugee family, the Menendez clan, to revive the Partagas label in the Dominican Republic. Meanwhile, Castro continued to use the hallowed Partagas name for his Cuban products; the only difference in the two countries' labels is that the Cuban brand says "Habana" at the bottom, while the Dominican label says "1845." Punch of Honduras and H. Upmann of the Dominican Republic are cursed with similar "shadow labels" in communist Cuba.

Above: The late Zino Davidoff, one of the premier cigar makers of the world, moved his operations from Cuba to the Dominican Republic in 1990. (Courtesy Davidoff of Geneva) Below: Drawing by Shanahan, © 1996 The New Yorker Magazine, Inc.

Cigars are now produced all over the world. Among the fine brands shown here are: Ashton, la Gloria Cubana, Park Lane, Avo, Partagas, Nat Sherman, Thomas Hinds, Juan Clemente, Romeo & Julieta, The Griffin, Licenciados, 898 Collection. Arturo Fuente, Habanica, Hoyo de Monterrey, Felipe Gregorio, Royal Jamaica, Joya de Nicaragua, Dunhill Aged, Davidoff, Julia Marlowe, and El Rico Habana. The lighters are by Alfred Dunhill; the cutter and ashtray are from Georgetown Tobacco. (Photo by Rick Bolen)

Zino Davidoff, the preeminent Geneva-based tobacco purveyor, was always identified with Cuban-grown tobacco, but in 1983 he introduced his "Zino" line of Honduran-made cigars to the

Shanahan

FROM *MILE ZERO*

by Thomas Sanchez (1989)

A buelo lost his heart the morning he saw Pearl his first day of work in the large cigar factory. He did not yet know she had stolen his heart. Abuelo thought he still had a choice in the matter. Pearl was one of the few women who worked in the cigar factory, the only woman on the third floor where Abuelo began his new job of Cigarmaker. Abuelo was not so much struck by Pearl's beauty, rather by the position she held in the factory. Most women labored in the lowly role of Stripper, who each day untied hundreds of *tercios*, bundled tobacco leaves barged from Havana. The women carefully stripped precious leaves from spiny stems, then pressed them between two boards to be sent on as wrappers to the Selectors. Never had Abuelo seen a female Selector. A Selector was an exalted position held by men with a keen sense of vision to distinguish the air-cured tobacco leaves by true color value. Perhaps Pearl inherited her extraordinary eyesight from her father, who could read the bottom of a storm-tossed sea. To watch Pearl's hands work quickly through stacks of tobacco leaves, eyes searching between colors ranging from golden papaya to ripe mahogany shading called *maduro*, was like witnessing a cat in a dark granary go about its stealthy nocturnal business of separating mice from mountains of wheat. Pearl did not work like a machine, rather as an adroit athlete laughing at a task made simple by exertion of inbred attributes. The creamy clove of garlic on Pearl's braided rope necklace rose and fell where her breasts began their full swell beneath a thin cotton dress. Pearl's skin glistened in the heat, her fingers flew, her eyes did not miss a trick. Blue clouds from the narrow cigars she continuously smoked swirled around her. Pearl appeared to exist in a haloed mist, struck by steady light cascading through lofty north-facing windows blocking fickle sea breezes which could disturb the cigarmakings so carefully laid out on the rowed tables of the great hall. Pearl's body exuded aromas fueling every man's desire high up in the third story of the cigar factory. The perfume of Pearl was a heady mixture of succulent reminiscences, of green dreams and urgent yearnings, of growing tobacco leaves hidden in slippery shade of muddied hillsides, of the pungent burnt scent of garlic rooted from firm earth.

BILANZ

DER FEIERLICHKEIT

Hugo Cloud, Bilanz der Feierlichkeit (Balance Sheet of Festivity), 1996, collage on newsprint, 16 ⅛ inches x 12 3/16 inches. (Modernism Gallery, San Francisco)

U. S. market and scored a bull's-eye. As production problems hobbled his Cuban production, in 1991 Davidoff boldly transferred all of his cigar industry to Santiago, Dominican Republic. Davidoff's move upset the myth that premium cigars had to come from Cuba. The new line of Davidoffs was initially marketed in the United States which, unlike Europe, was not hopelessly entranced by the Cuban spell. Davidoff ardently courted American smokers by opening posh stores in New York and Beverly Hills. Though his

new cigars were not as spicy and rich as the Cuban tobacco, they suited American tastebuds. "They are excellently made high quality cigars which do not fight you when you smoke them," said Davidoff to Paul Garmirian of Georgetown Tobacco.

Today, the Dominican Republic is the world's leading producer of premium cigars, with 50 million of their handmade cigars destined annually for the United States. It has a climate similar to Cuba and excellent soil and rainfall patterns for tobacco. Cigars are manufactured all over the world, from the Philippines and Indonesia to Mexico, Brazil, and the Canary Islands, as well as in Italy, Holland, Denmark, and Germany. The novelist Stendhal smoked Toscanis, manufactured in Italy. "On a cold morning in winter, " he wrote," a Tuscan cigar fortifies the soul." Dryly rolled, they have a powerful smell.

Opposite: Stuart Davis, Magazine and Cigar, *1931, oil on canvas, 12 x 16 inches. An art critic for the* Philadelphia Record *wrote: "It is a detective magazine, beside which reposes an unsmoked and extremely black cigar—the kind that had best remain unsmoked." (Richard York Gallery, New York)*

It is safe to generalize that the finest cigars in the world come from countries near Cuba. Nicaraguan cigars like the Joya de Nicaragua, and Mexican varities such as Te-Amo, usually have a strong perfume and a peppery scent. The American connoisseur Paul Garmirian makes a very fine cigar in Santiago, Dominican Republic.

The Nicaraguan cigar industry flourished until the *Sandinista* revolution left cultivation and production in turmoil but is now back on its feet. Brands such as Mexico's Te-Amo and the Dominican Republic's Don Diego and H. Upmann have varied in quality over the years, but are generally good smokes. The consistent winners seem to be Macanudo of Jamaica and Partagas of the Dominican Republic. The brands Montecruz, Flamenco, Don Diego, and Don Miguel landed in the Canary Islands, producing well-made if milder smokes.

Dominican Republic cigars use wrappers grown in Connecticut, Cameroon, Nicaragua, Ecuador, Brazil, and Mexico. The sandy loam of the Connecticut River Valley has ideal chemistry and composition for producing the high-grade wrapper leaves called Connecticut Shade. Macanudo and Davidoff use Connecticut Shade wrappers around Jamaican and Dominican fillers. These Yankee tobacco plants, grown from the Hazelwood strain of Cuban seed, are cultivated under 10-foot high cheesecloth tents that shade the plants from harsh sun rays. The growing cycle begins in March with harvest in August. Costly production has this tobacco selling for as much as $40 a pound, adding roughly 50 cents to the price of each cigar wrapped in it. Cuban tobacco may still be the best for filler, but, curiously, the island still has not produced the best wrapper leaves. However, in 1995 they just harvested their first batch planted with seed from Connecticut Shade.

CHAPTER SIX

WOMEN AND CIGARS

"A cigar numbs sorrow and fills the solitary hours with a million gracious images."

GEORGE SAND, 1867

In the 1958 film version of Colette's novella *Gigi*, the playful Parisian coquette was trained to be the perfect woman; among myriad social skills, she was taught to select a fine cigar, clip it, and present it to a gentleman. "Once a woman understands the tastes of a man, cigars included, and once a man knows what pleases a woman, they may said to be well matched," wrote the author. The film went further, having Leslie Caron smelling and then rolling cigars next to her ear to determine quality. Study and know the cigar, yes, but—God forbid—a girl wasn't supposed to actually smoke it herself!

Today, women from New York to San Francisco are getting together and smoking. Diana Silvius, owner of the Up Down Tobacco Shop in Chicago and board member of the Tobacconist's Association of America, feels that women are the next big market for cigars, and the numbers are growing. Julie Ross co-founded the George Sand Society of Santa Monica, a cigar club for women (and men), which now has a chapter in Manhattan. Her interest in cigars was sparked by a European friend who thought it perfectly natural to smoke a cigar in a cafe or after dinner—and not just to mimic men. After all, women in Italy regularly smoke cigars, while large numbers smoke in Holland and Denmark. The George Sand Society of Santa Monica is about two-thirds women. In an unusual twist,

In a reversal of cigar stereotypes of the West, women of the Ami tribe in Formosa consider big cigars feminine and small cigars masculine. (Bettmann Archive)

Tobacos Esquisitos label

Above: George Sand smoked cigars because she liked them and dressed like a man because the clothes were comfortable and allowed her to observe humanity from a different perspective. (Culver Pictures)

women are taking their husbands and male friends to the dinner events and introducing them to the pleasures of the cigar. Molly Gleason, a San Francisco real estate broker and Bay Area party organizer, gathers women cigar smokers at that city's Alfred Dunhill shop and at the Cypress Club Restaurant. Gleason, who carries a cigar clipper in her wallet and keeps a log entry on each cigar she smokes, says women have to stop thinking of cigar smoking as treading on Sacred Male Turf. "Turf is like a conversation, it is constantly being redefined and shared." Although she smokes for the pleasure of the cigar itself, she admits that "it's a magnet for men, which is something I don't mind."

A number of notable comediennes have found their way to the humidors. The late Lucille Ball relished cigars; Bette Midler confesses to the pleasure. Actress Whoopi Goldberg first smoked cheap cigars as a teenager, but with a string of film successes behind her, she's now smoking Cohibas and the 80 Anniversario, the hard-to-find Cuban Davidoff created to

Opposite: Leslie Caron and Robert Jourdain in Gigi, 1958. (Corbis/ Bettmann) Below: Madonna lit up on the David Letterman Show in 1994. (AP Photo/ Wide World Photos)

celebrate the late Zino Davidoff's 80th birthday. Super model Linda Evangelista, cover girl for *Cigar Aficionado*, admits to being a cigar fan, but a lightweight, "I love the Cohiba robusto, but I can't do the whole thing." Madonna puffed a huge cigar on the David Letterman show in 1994, but purists of *los puros* question whether or not she genuinely likes them, or merely intended

Alexandra's

occasional puff...

Alexandra Weems, Alexandra's
Occasional Puff, 1995, ink on
paperboard, 12 x 9¹/₂ inches.
(Alexandra Weems, New York)

to upstage one of television's better known cigar smokers. (Letterman himself is now no longer allowed to smoke on camera.) Sharon Stone, Demi Moore, Ellen Barkin, and Jodie Foster light up.

Actually, not until the nineteenth century did cigar and pipe smoking become "gender-specific" to men. John Cockburn, an English traveler to Costa Rica, wrote in 1735, "These gentlemen gave us some seegars . . . these are leaves of tobacco rolled up in such a manner that they serve both for a pipe and for tobacco itself. These the ladies, as well as the gentlemen, are very fond of smoking."

By some accounts, in the eighteenth century men and women in America and Europe smoked in nearly equal numbers. This changed in the nineteenth century when the smoking club became the domain of the Victorian gentleman. Still, there were notable exceptions. Amandine Aurore Lucie Dupin, baroness Dudevant—better known as the novelist George Sand—was the most noted woman cigar smoker. There was also the princess of Metternich, the animal painter Rosa Bonheur, and Lizst's mistress Marie d'Agoult (who wrote under the name Daniel Stern)—all lovers of the rolled leaf. The American poetess Amy Lowell became so alarmed at the approach of World War I that she stockpiled 10,000 Filipino cigars in case of a shortage. (Manila produces some fine cigars, including La Flor de la Isabela. Spanish sailors took Cuban tobacco seed to these islands in the sixteenth century.)

In the past, women who smoked cigars were seen as eccentric and sexually renegade. According to Richard Klein, author of *Cigarettes Are Sublime* (1993): " . . . a woman smoking a cigar sent a signal that she had assumed the male prerogative of taking pleasure in public. And so cigars were props for women who staged their sexuality in public—gypsies, actresses and prostitutes."

(Woodfin Camp, New York)

"THE BETROTHED" *'You must choose between me and your cigar.'*

by Rudyard Kipling, from *Departmental Ditties* (1890)

Open the old cigar-box, get me a Cuba stout,
For things are running crossways, and Maggie and
    I are out.

We quarrelled about Havanas—we fought o'er a
    good cheroot,
And I know she is exacting, and she says I am a
    brute.

Open the old cigar-box—let me consider a space;
In the soft blue veil of the vapour musing on
    Maggie's face.

Maggie is pretty to look at—Maggie's a loving lass,
But the prettiest cheeks must wrinkle, the truest of
    loves must pass.

There's peace in a Laranaga, there's calm in a
    Henry Clay,
But the best cigar in an hour is finished and
    thrown away—

Thrown away for another as perfect and ripe and
    brown—
But I could not throw away Maggie for fear o' the
    talk o' the town!

Maggie, my wife at fifty—grey and dour and old—
With never another Maggie to purchase for love or
    gold!

And the light of Days that have Been the dark of
    the Days that Are,
And Love's torch stinking and stale, like the butt
    of a dead cigar—

The butt of a dead cigar you are bound to keep in
    your pocket—
With never a new one to light tho' it's charred and
    black to the socket.

Open the old cigar-box—let me consider a while
Here is a mild Manila—there is a wifely smile.

Which is the better portion—bondage bought
    with a ring,
Or a harem of dusky beauties fifty tied in a string?

Counsellors cunning and silent—comforters true
    and tried,
And never a one of the fifty to sneer at a rival
    bride.

Thought in the early morning, solace in time of
    woes,
Peace in the hush of the twilight, balm ere my
    eyelids close,

This will the fifty give me, asking nought in
    return,
With only a *Suttee's* passion—to do their duty and
    burn.

This will the fifty give me. When they are spent and dead,
Five times other fifties shall be my servants instead.

The furrows of far-off Java, the isles of the Spanish Main,
When they hear that my harem is empty will send me my brides again.

I will take no heed to their raiment, nor food for their mouths withal,
So long as the gulls are nesting, so long as the showers fall.

I will scent 'em with best Vanilla, with tea will I temper their hides,
And the Moor and the Mormon shall envy who read of the tale of my brides.

For Maggie has written a letter to give me my choice between
The wee little whimpering Love and the great god Nick o' Teen.

And I have been servant of Love for barely a twelve-month clear,
But I have been Priest of Partagas a matter of seven year;

And the gloom of my bachelor days is flecked with the cheery light
Of stumps that I burned to Friendship and Pleasure and Work and Fight.

And I turn my eyes to the future that Maggie and I must prove,
But the only light on the marshes is the Will-o'-the-Wisp of Love.

Will it see me safe through my journey or leave me bogged in the mire?
Since a puff of tobacco can cloud it, shall I follow the fitful fire?

Open the old cigar-box—let me consider anew—
Old friends, and who is Maggie that I should abandon *you*?

A million surplus Maggies are willing to bear the yoke;
And a woman is only a woman, but a good cigar is a Smoke.

Light me another Cuba—I hold to my first-sworn vows,
If Maggie will have no rival, I'll have no Maggie for Spouse!

Opposite: Film star Edward G. Robinson and his wife shared a public cigar and a private joke before getting on a train. (Culver Pictures)

One thinks of Bizet's brazen heroine, Carmen, who works in a Sevilla cigar factory and defiantly smokes in the town square. In America we had Bonnie Parker, who smoked cigars, wrote poetry, and robbed banks with Clyde Parker. Marlene Dietrich wore men's clothes in the 1930s and smoked cigars at the Stork Club with her buddy Ernest Hemingway. French novelist Colette also smoked.

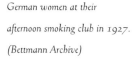

Cigar smoking has had female foes for as long as cigars have been smoked. There is the famous Rudyard Kipling poem "The Betrothed" (1899) in which a young woman tells her husband-to-be, "Darling, you must choose between me and your cigars." In the end the man does make a choice and says, "A woman is just a woman, but a cigar is a smoke." Did Kipling really mean that as simplistically sexist as it sounds? Perhaps, but it might easily be said by a woman about a man—one can't always count on the opposite sex to provide happiness and well-being forever.

Opposite: Gus Heinze, Neon Cigars #293, 1995, acrylic on gesso panel, 18 x 22 inches. (Modernism Gallery, San Francisco)

German women at their afternoon smoking club in 1927. (Bettmann Archive)

CHAPTER SEVEN

HOW TO CHOOSE AND SMOKE A CIGAR

". . . I promised myself that if ever I had some money that I would savor a cigar each day after lunch and dinner. This is the only resolution of my youth that I have kept, and the only realized ambition which has not brought disillusion."

SOMERSET MAUGHAM, *THE SUMMING UP*

There is no such thing as the perfect cigar, but with experimentation, you will find cigars that are right for you. How to start? Plunge in. Go to a good tobacconist with a humidor room and pick out some cigars. Connoisseurship evolves through trial and error. My advice would be to start at the medium to top price range, and purchase only cigars that are totally made by hand. You may occasionally be surprised by lesser brands, but if you're looking for quality, avoid all machine-made cigars.

If you're in a shop outside the United States, you can purchase Cubans. Remember to smoke them there, or risk running afoul of U.S. Customs. First, look at the box. In the past, the words *Hecho a Mano* meant cigars completely made by hand and simply *Hecho a Cuba* indicated

The first Alfred Dunhill shop at 31 A Duke Street, London, in 1907. (The Alfred Dunhill Archive Collection)

machine-made. Today, that is no longer the case. *Hecho a Mano* can mean that only the wrapper has been rolled by hand over a machine-made filler and binder. Accept nothing less than *Totalemente a mano*.

Top-named brands in large sizes such as the Churchill are usually well made and well inspected even when packed in tubes, but smaller-sized cigars in tubes—even a box bearing a famous name like H. Upmann or Romeo y Julieta— are not scrutinized as carefully by their manufacturer as those

Opposite: Philip Guston, Untitled (Figure Smoking), *1969, acrylic on panel, 24 x 26 ¹/₂ inches (Private Collection, London/Courtesy McKee Gallery, New York)*

A custom humidor of purpleheart wood inlaid with sterling silver, built for the Tosca Cafe in San Franciso by Peter Ridet in 1995. (Photo by Rick Bolen)

packed "nude" in a box. They may vary in color as well as in quality. Ask to examine the cigars, even if it means having the salesperson open the box. In fact, you should always examine a box before buying it. Roll a cigar between your fingers; it should be firm but moistly resilient enough to spring back without the sound of cracking tobacco. Don't accept any cigars that are brittle to the touch or whose wrappers are damaged in any way. Reject cigars with large veins, discoloration, or spots.

Another good place to experiment is with mail order catalogues. The most amusing is J.R. of Statesville, North Carolina, where owner Lew Rothman spouts jokes and offers great cigars in a whirlwind manner. I also like Thompson's of Tampa, and Smokin' Joe's Tobacco of Knoxville, Tennessee. Or call a well-known cigar shop such as Nat Sherman in Manhattan, Davidoff in Los Angeles, Georgetown Tobacco in Washington, D.C., or Alfred Dunhill in San Francisco. Cigar bars like Hamilton's in Los Angeles, the Occidental Grill in San Francisco, or Lexington Bar and Books in New York also have humidors.

Cigars come in different sizes and are measured by ring gauges based on $^1/_{64}$ of an inch. Thus a ring gauge of 42 would be $^{42}/_{64}$ of an inch in diameter. The larger ring gauge cigars have a fuller taste and a cooler, smoother draw. In your initial taste tests, start out with smaller cigars in a mild blend such as Macanudo or Hoyo de Monterrey. Working from mild to full-bodied cigars allows your tastebuds to respond to the increasing taste sensation, much as wine drinkers start with Chardonnay and end up with a dark Bordeaux. Cigars with dark leaf wrappers—called *maduro*—have a higher sugar content and are usually full-bodied spicy cigars with a sweet taste. These are my personal favorites.

Good Havana cigars go through three fermentations before they are rolled, and

FROM THE AUTOBIOGRAPHY OF MARK TWAIN

(Bettmann Archive)

I had not smoked for three full months and no words can adequately describe the smoke appetite that was consuming me. I had been a smoker from my ninth year—a private one during the first two years but a public one after that—that is to say, after my father's death. I was smoking and utterly happy before I was thirty steps from the lodge door. I do not now know what the brand of the cigar was. It was probably not choice, or the previous smoker would not have thrown it away so soon. But I realized that it was the best cigar that was ever made. The previous smoker would have thought the same if he had been without a smoke for three months. I smoked that stub without shame. I could not do it now without shame, because now I am more refined than I was then. But I would smoke it just the same. I know myself and I know the human race well enough to know that.

In those days the native cigar was so cheap that a person who could afford anything could afford cigars. Mr. Garth had a great tobacco factory and he also had a small shop in the village for the retail sale of his products. He had one brand of cigars which even poverty itself was able to buy. He had had these in stock a good many years and although they looked well enough on the outside, their insides had decayed to dust and would fly out like a puff of vapor when they were broken in two. This brand was very popular on account of its extreme cheapness. Mr. Garth had other brands which were cheap and some that were bad, but the supremacy over them enjoyed by this brand was indicated by its name. It was called "Garth's damnedest." We used to trade old newspapers (exchanges) for that brand.

There was another shop in the village where the conditions were friendly to penniless boys. It was kept by a lonely and melancholy little hunchback and we could always get a supply of cigars by fetching a bucket of water for him from the village pump, whether he needed water or not. One day we found him asleep in his chair—a custom of his—and we waited patiently for him to wake up, which was a custom of ours. But he slept so long this time that at last our patience was exhausted and we tried to wake him—but he was dead. I remember the shock of it yet.

they continue to develop after they have been placed in a box, much as fine wines do. A good cigar store knows that recently rolled cigars should be sold within weeks after they are boxed and shipped if they are to be smoked as "fresh" cigars; otherwise they should not be sold for at least twelve months. They should be stored in a humidor so that they ripen properly. This is much like the difference between a Nouveau Beaujolais wine, which should be consumed as soon as it is produced, and a vintage wine that needs aging. Likewise, just as some wines turn to vinegar after a decade or two, certain cigars should be smoked within a decade of production, while some pre-Castro cigars remain marvelous today.

Once you have a selection of cigars, plan an afternoon or evening when you have two or three free hours—you don't want to rush this. Smoke with a friend, and you'll be able to compare taste sensations. Pick out two or three cigars of different brands and sample them; just smoke half or less, take a break, and then try another. Between cigars try a little red wine, port, or cognac, or something refreshing such as lemon sherbet or fruit juice to cleanse your palate.

With a handmade cigar you need to clip or cut the *head*, the closed end, before lighting. The cigar label is always closest to the head. The end you light is called the *foot*. Use a pair of cigar scissors or a "guillotine" clipper to snip about an $^1/8$ of an inch

Eugene Beck, The Cigar Bearers, *1978, etching, 3 $^1/_2$ x 5 $^1/_2$ inches. (Modernism Gallery, San Francisco)*

off the top—no more. (I find the guillotine the easiest to use, and it slips easily into your pocket.) In a pinch you can use a very sharp knife or even your teeth, though this is usually frowned upon except in western saloons. Some people like to cut a V shape in the head or to poke a hole in the wrapper with a spike (which I do not recommend). Your main concern should be to avoid tearing the wrapper leaf; this may happen if the cigar is too dry or if you guillotine it clumsily.

Now, to light the cigar. In the old days there was a tradition of gently running a flame down the length of a cigar to burn off the heavy gum adhesive, which some Spanish rollers used to hold the wrapper in place. This hasn't been necessary for years because of the improved vegetable-based gums. So don't do it.

Smaller cigars will light easily with one match, but with Churchills, for example, you'll need a little preparation. Before putting it in your mouth, hold the cigar horizontally in your hand and rotate the foot over a match flame for a few seconds until it is evenly burning. Use a second or third match if necessary. (Actually, a butane lighter or wood shavings are the best.) Now place the cigar in your mouth, and lightly draw smoke into your mouth. If it still isn't lit, apply the match and draw until the cigar is lit. Don't use too much flame or you'll cause the cigar to burn too fast and overheat, which may alter the taste.

Don't inhale the smoke or you'll be coughing. Cigar smoke is meant to be savored in the mouth and then released, much the way a wine taster will take a mouthful of wine and then expel it without swallowing.

To remove the band or not? The French poet Stéphane Mallarmé recalled the voluptuousness of a lunch with his father in the last century: "After finishing the meal, he produced boxes of sparkling cigars: Valle, Clay, Upmann. I opened these boxes which evoked visions of dancing girls, and I removed the bands, because that is what is to be done." English etiquette also calls for removing the band. A number of restaurants will remove the band after you've selected a cigar from the humidor. In Germany it is customary to leave the label on. Most American tobacconists tell customers that band removal is optional. Zino Davidoff called it a "personal choice." He used to remove the band only after the cigar was well lit and "running." Anwer Bati, author of *The Cigar*

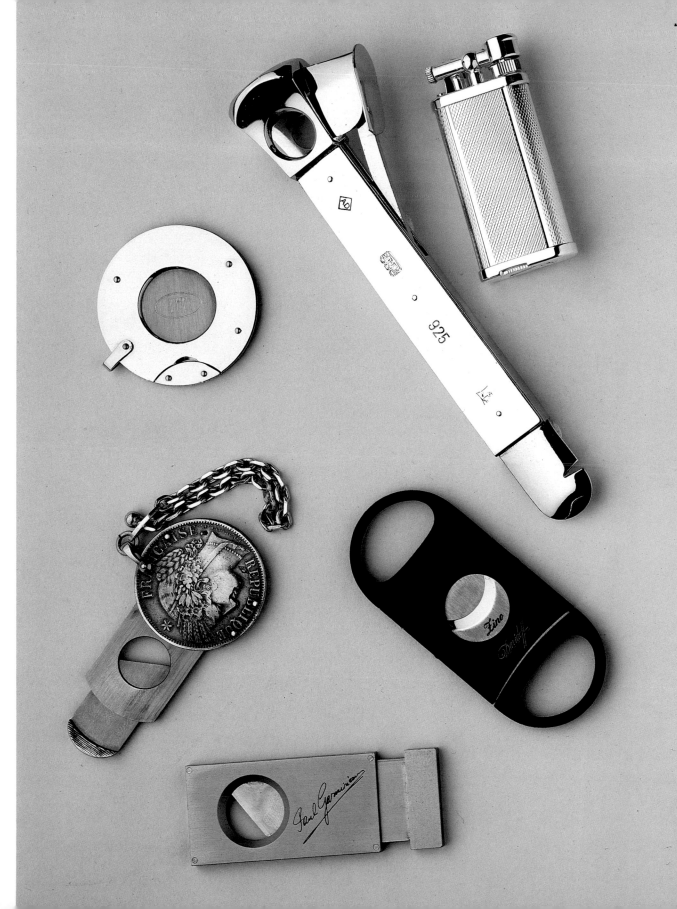

Companion, concurs, suggesting the removal after the cigar has heated up enough to soften its adhesive so that it peels off without tearing the delicate wrapper leaf. "In any case," writes Davidoff, ever the sensualist, "the cigar is even more attractive in its nudity."

Opposite: The Bolivar, one of the great Cuban brands, was named for the revolutionary who led independence wars in the present nations of Venezuela, Colombia, Panama, Ecuador, Peru, and Bolivia. (Photo by Rick Bolen)

No matter what country you are in, if you've been offered a cigar with the band on, leave it on, if you so please. Cigar bands are among the most beautiful printed design accents in life, and aficionados enjoy looking at them just as they do the labels of wine bottles. In the world of cigars, for all its susceptibility to pretension, it still comes down to whether you're enjoying a good smoke.

The cigar should be held firmly in the mouth, but don't clench it in your teeth, chew the end, or drool over it. As George Brightman of *Cigar Aficionado* once, said, "If you kiss a cigar—it will kiss you back. If you treat it like a dog—it will turn around and bite you." Try to keep the cigar from becoming too moist from saliva, if only to spare your companions an unattractive sight. Forget cigar holders; they are absurd. As Davidoff said, "Would you want to drink a good wine with a straw?" Smoke slowly, taking no more than two puffs a minute lest the cigar become overheated, which will sour the taste. Depending on the size, a cigar should last between 30 minutes and one and one-half hours to smoke, generally about 50 puffs. August Barthélemy, author of *L'Art de fumer pipe et cigare* (1849), noted that "The true smoker abstains from imitating Vesuvius." In other words, the cigar should spend more time in your hand or in the ashtray than in your mouth. As Davidoff so wisely said, "A cigar ought not to be smoked solely with the mouth, but with the hand, the eyes, and with the spirit."

A German cigar ad from the 1930s. (Deco Deluxe, New York)

The smoke is not to be inhaled into the lungs but held in the mouth for a few seconds, allowing the tongue and upper palate to savor the different aromas. Cigar tobacco has less nicotine than cigarettes and burns cooler, but it can produce a mild intoxication or excitement (one of the reasons Freud and other great minds smoked while they wrote). The first half of the cigar is always the best in taste and lowest in nicotine; the stronger, sometimes less pleasant vapors and tars are produced as the cigar burns down to a hot stub.

Superstition shrouds the ash. Some people believe the ash acts as a kind of thermostat or radiator to keep the cigar burning cooler. It doesn't. It serves no purpose save being beautiful to look at. A long, evenly formed gray ash generally indicates a well-constructed hand made cigar, but don't make too much of it. Let it fall off naturally in an ashtray rather than tapping it off as with a cigarette.

Drawing by Robert Grossman.
(©1996 The New York Times)

Robert Grossman

Trial lawyer Clarence Darrow, an avid cigar smoker usually associated with just causes and fair play, was not above using his ash to distract a jury while opposing lawyers made closing arguments. Before lighting up, he would push a thin steel wire length-wise through the cigar, which then supported an ash nearly as long as the original cigar. Holding it prominently in view of the jury while feigning absorption in his opponents presentations, Darrow invariably distracted the jurors who, waiting for his unbelievably long ash to fall any second, paid little attention to the case at hand.

To extinguish a cigar, simply place it in an ashtray, and it will expire on its own in a minute or two. There is no need to crush it. Since a dead cigar emits an odor far less appealing than a burning one, you should dispose of it quickly, even if you plan to smoke another. Refresh your mouth with a beverage and wait a few minutes before you light up your next. As Eugene Marsan wrote in *Le Cigare*, "Two cigars on top of each other reveal an obsession or a brutality of the soul."

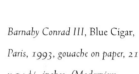

Traditional wisdom advises smoking milder cigars in the morning and afternoon, reserving stronger ones for after dinner. The lighter-colored cigar, called a *claro* and *colorado claro*, is generally milder than those made with dark *colorado*, *maduro*, or *oscuro* wrappers. There is a light green-colored cigar known as a *double claro* or *clarissimo*, but do not make the mistake of believing it is necessarily a "fresh" or recently rolled cigar. It is simply a light cigar that has been wrapped in a leaf that received special treatment during growing and picking. Inside the filler will be darker. The maduro leaves are picked higher up on the tobacco plant—where they receive more intense sunlight—and are allowed to ferment longer to produce a pungent spicy taste.

Contrary to what some say, it is all right to relight your cigar if it goes out, but usually only if less than half of it has been smoked. If it does go out, knock off the ashes, scrape out the end with a match or even your car keys, hold a flame to the cigar as you rotate it in your hand, then resume smoking. (On the other hand, a cigar should not be relit the next day; it becomes foul after a few hours.) If a cigar is hard to "draw" on or if it goes out more than two or three times before you've smoked a third of it, it may have been wrapped too tightly. Throw it out and try another.

What to drink with a cigar? Chefs and taste experts have spent years matching cigars with different beverages. The traditional favorites are port, wine, brandy and cognac. On a hot day, a cold lager beer goes well. For those who prefer non-alcoholic beverages, try a well-made espresso or fresh fruit juice.

Bernard le Roy and Maurice Szafran note in their lavish book *The Illustrated History of Cigars* (1993) that a number of French chefs have paired specific cigars with specific wines. For example, the founder of the French Institute of Taste, Jacques Puisais, thinks a corona by El Rey del Mundo is perfect with a white Chateauneuf-du-

Opposite: A fine wood and sterling ashtray made by David Linley for Alfred Dunhill, David Linley's cigar case, and Alfred Dunhill's sterling lighter. (Photo by Rick Bolen)

Barnaby Conrad III, Blue Cigar, Paris, 1993, gouache on paper, 21 x 14 1/2 inches. (Modernism Gallery, San Francisco)

Pape. According to Jean Bardet, a well-known chef from Tours, an ideal combination would be an Epicure by Hoyo de Monterrey with the fruity bouquet of a Gewürztraminer.

The great Zino Davidoff created the Chateau Haut-Brion, Lafite, Margaux, and Mouton line of cigars to complement the rich dark Bordeaux vintages. He further named an extremely mild cigar the Dom Perignon for the great champagne.

Opposite: The great Mexican artist Diego Rivera painted this cubist gem, Still Life with Cigar, in Paris in 1916. Note the cigar with the French tri-color band. (Private collection/Art Resource, New York)

For cocktails and liqueurs, I turned to Dale DeGroff, beverage manager of Manhattan's Rainbow Room, who likes a pre-dinner cigar, and often pairs a Montecristo with a Manhattan cocktail or the older bourbons. For after dinner, DeGroff's favorite is Arturo Fuente's OpusX or the Gloria Cubana with an aged

Armagnac. Dr. Robert Rothberg, director of The Scotch Malt Whisky Society of America, favors the OpusX with whiskies such as The Macallan or Ben Nevis which have been matured in a sherry cask. The doctor also pairs the Los Indios brand with classic Orkney brands like Highland Park and with the famed Isla names Lephroig and Lagavulin.

Cigars vary tremendously in size. The smallest Havana ever made was the Corona made by Bolívar, called the Delgado, which was only one and one-quarter inches long, while the largest was a Panatella at over 19 inches. Before World War II the Henry Clay company produced a monster Havana cigar over six feet long known as the Koh-I-Noor. Presented to an Indian Maharajah, it is now on exhibit at the Tobacco Museum in Bunde, Germany.

A cigar as small as a Delgado strikes me as inhospitable as serving a sparrow on Thanksgiving. If you want a small cigar, try the petit Corona which is about three inches long and thick enough to provide good flavor. There are many theories on what size cigar a man should smoke according to his body type. Paul Garmirian says a short heavy man should not smoke a huge Churchill because it would dwarf him; nor should a big man smoke a tiny cheroot. I say smoke whatever size you like.

The Corona at five and a half inches long is an ideal all-around cigar size. From there we move to the Lonsdale—which is a bit over six inches long—a typical cigar size for someone wanting a long smoke. Edward VII, Churchill, and King Farouk were partial to the Double Corona, which runs eight to nine inches long. Financier Steve Worthington says that during a tough negotiation he'll start with a small cigar in the first hour, then light a "solid Churchillian rocket fuel booster" to let them know he has staying power. I personally like the distinctive Pyramid shape with its tapered shape.

To care for your cigars properly, you need a humidor. Depending on your needs, this can range from a box the size of a shaving kit to a walk-in closet. The important thing is to keep the cigars at a temperature of 68 to 72 degrees with humidity at 60 to 70 percent. In a pinch you can use the wooden cigar box itself by removing one of the cigars on the bottom and replacing it with a glass tube open at either end that has been stuffed with a moist sponge, available at good cigar stores. These should be moistened once a month. A cigar that has gone dry can be revived with a few weeks "convalescence" in a good humidor, but beware

John Register, Eugene, 1995, oil on canvas, 18 x 18 inches. (Modernism Gallery, San Francisco)

of "drowning" a cigar in too much moisture. Under no circumstances store cigars in a refrigerator, whether in boxes or plastic bags.

In general, humidors are nearly airtight boxes made of walnut or oak and lined with fine cedar. They range in price from $200 for a simple one to $5,000 for art objects such as those made by Queen Elizabeth's nephew, Lord Linley, and sold at Alfred Dunhill. J. C. Pendergast of Racine, Wisconsin, makes some of the best humidors in the world at the most reasonable prices.

Opposite: Marcel Duchamp at the Los Angeles County Museum in 1963, photographed by Julian Wasser. (Julian Wasser, Los Angeles)

Many fine cigars are sold in aluminum tubes. These are convenient for safely transporting cigars in a coat pocket, but not for storage. Paul Garmirian left H. Upmanns and Romeo y Julietas in their original tubes for a year and then tested them, finding them tired and dull. Happily, after placing them in a humidor where he rotated them regularly, he found that they came back to life. When you buy tubed cigars, immediately take them out of the tube and put them in a humidor.

Cigar etiquette naturally takes into account people who do not like cigars. Where and when to smoke? "There is nothing more agreeable than having a place where one can throw on the floor as many cigar butts as one pleases without the subconscious fear of a maid who is waiting like a sentinel to place an ashtray where the ashes are going to fall," wrote Fidel Castro in his book *Letters from Gaol*. It is unlikely that you will have such freedom unless you end up in a Cuban jail or camp out in the Gobi Desert. It has certainly become more difficult to know when it is proper to smoke. Always ask in a private home or restaurant, and in both cases be prepared to step outside for that smoke or wait until you get home, before acting on the immortal words of Edward VII, "Gentlemen, you may smoke."

I'll end this book with older words still, from Thackeray's wonderful *Vanity Fair:* "I am done—pay the bills and get me a cigar."

Man Ray, Old Marcel (Anselmino 20), *1972, from the portfolio* Monument à Christophe Colomb et à Marcel Duchamp, *Edition of 125, etching and aquatint, 10 x 9 7/8 inches. The smoke from the cigar spells "rrose," referring to surrealist Duchamp's punning alter-ego Rrose Selavy. (Modernism Gallery, San Francisco)*

SELECTED BIBLIOGRAPHY

Auster, Paul. *Smoke & Blue in the Face: Two Films*. New York: Hyperion, 1995.

Bati, Anwer. *The Cigar Companion*. Philadephia: Running Press, 1993.

Cigar Aficionado, Vol. 1–4, 1992-1996. New York: M. Shanken Communications, Inc.

Davidoff, Zino. *The Connoisseur's Book of the Cigar*. New York: McGraw Hill, 1969.

Davidson, Joe. *The Art of the Cigar Label*. Edison, New Jersey: The Wellfleet Press, 1989.

Edmark, Tomima, *Cigar Chic*. Arlington, Texas: The Summit Publishing Group, 1995.

Garmirian, Paul B. K. *The Gourmet Guide to Cigars*. McLean, Virginia: Cedar Publications, 1990.

Hacker, Richard Carleton.*The Ultimate Cigar Book*. Beverly Hills, California: Autumngold Publishing, 1993.

Infante, Cabrera G. *Holy Smoke*. London: Faber and Faber, 1985.

Jiménez, Antonio Nuñez. *The Journey of the Havana Cigar*. Neptune City, New Jersey: T.F.H. Publications, Inc., 1988.

Le Roy, Bernard, and Maurice Szafran. *The Illustrated History of Cigars*. London: Harold Starke Publishers Limited, 1993.

Opposite: Mark Adams, Cigar Boxes, 1996, watercolor, $21^{1}/_{2}$ x $23^{1}/_{2}$ inches. (John Berggruen Gallery, San Francisco)

Grateful acknowledgment is made for permission to reprint excerpts from the following:

Holy Smoke, by G. Cabrera Infante. Copyright © 1985 by G. Cabrera Infante. Reprinted with permission by Faber and Faber.

Mile Zero, by Thomas Sanchez. Copyright ©1989 by Thomas Sanchez. Reprinted with permission by Alfred A. Knopf, Inc.

The Connoisseur's Book of the Cigar, by Zino Davidoff. Copyright © 1969 by Zino Davidoff. Reprinted with permission by McGraw-Hill.

The Idiot, by Fyodor Dostoyevsky. Translation copyright © 1993 by Henry Carlisle and Olga Carlisle. Reprinted with permission of Penguin USA.

INDEX

Following page: The late George Burns celebrated his 100th birthday in 1996. (UPI/Bettmann)

REPUBLICA DE CUBA

NAT SHERMAN

25 TOROS **25**
HAND MADE

R

HOYO DE MONTERREY
Double Corona
English Market Selection

Suntouso   Hecho A Ma

TABACOS DE PARTAGAS Y Cª · 1845 · FLOR DE TABACOS DE

PARTAGAS
25 - DUNHILL SELECCION SUPREMA No. 12

FLOR DE TABACOS DE PARTAGAS Y CA · 1845

MONTECRIS

DE TABACOS DE PARTAGAS Y Cª · HABANA · FLOR ACOS DE PAR

PARTAGAS
25 · LUSITANIA

La Habana, Cuba

CRUZ 25 DUNHILL NATURAL
CLARO Nº 220

ROMEO Y JULIETA
25 · PERFECTOS

HOYO
DE MONTERREY

REPU

ONTECRISTO   25 · Montecristo No. 5   HABANA

H. UPMANN
25 · LONSDALES

· R · J ·
PARK LANE

TELEGRAPH

HABANA   HABANA   HABANA

PUNCH

BOLIVAR
25 · CORONAS GIGANTES Made by Hand

BOLIVAR   BOLIVAR   BOLIVAR